CHRISTIAN PACIFISM IN HISTORY

D0440905

BY THE SAME AUTHOR

VISIBLE SAINTS: THE CONGREGATIONAL WAY,
    1640–60

THE HOLY SPIRIT IN PURITAN FAITH AND
    EXPERIENCE

THE HOLY SPIRIT AND OURSELVES

THE FAITH OF DANTE ALIGHIERI

RICHARD BAXTER

THE PURITAN SPIRIT, ESSAYS AND ADDRESSES

THE WELSH SAINTS, 1640–1660

HOWEL HARRIS, 1714–1773

The first three titles listed above are currently
out of print but may be available from a library.

Geoffrey F. Nuttall has been elected President of
the (British) Ecclesiastical History Society, 1972–
73.

Connie Dyer

Christian Pacifism in History

By

GEOFFREY F. NUTTALL, D.D.

Lecturer in Church History, New College, London

WORLD WITHOUT WAR COUNCIL

CONCORDIA UNIVERSITY LIBRAR
PORTLAND, OR 97211

©copyright Basil Blackwell & Mott, Ltd. 1958

Reprinted by arrangement with Basil Blackwell & Mott, Ltd., November, 1971

Printed in the United States

World Without War Council

1730 Grove Street, Berkeley, California 94709

FOREWORD

THIS LITTLE VOLUME originating in a series of lectures more than a dozen years ago at York, England, is deceptively unpretentious. It deserves reprinting. It represents a widely neglected phase of the insistent contemporary problem, viz., the cardinal element in the gospel by which the acceptability or unacceptability of war for the Christian is to be determined. Looking at the matter historically as a historian of the Church, Professor Nuttall shows that the answers at different times have been different and that no one of them has been always prominent. Hence today the issue is not usually drawn with any consensus as to just where the decisive factor is to be found. That may be because both war and the Gospel have each a variety of aspects or concomitants that prevent a simplistic moral analysis. Taking five historical manifestations of group Christian pacifism, the author leads us from the first century to the twentieth with well documented evidence of their different emphases, all leading, however, in some minor group to radical conscientious repudiation of war. In each instance that negative repudiation is the reflection of a different and positive religious loyalty and affirmation. Beside the pacifism of the early Church, that of the medieval sects, the reformation groups of Anabaptists and Mennonites on the Continent and the Quakers in England is dealt with.

Ever since the days of Constantine the Church as a whole has accepted war. Its reasons for doing so must have been as various as the reasons of the pacifist minority. It is the latter, however, which is the illuminating central topic of the pages that follow.

What has been for the mentality of one period or one group adequate for acceptance or rejection of war may be quite alien to another viewpoint. Neither side at the present time seems to have focussed effectively on a contemporary statement of the issue. The grounds producing pacifist Christians in all five of Dr. Nuttall's periods may still all be valid. They do not cancel each other out. But the reader is left, whether he begins with a prejudice in favor of or against the pacifist position, to search for the element or elements in our understanding of the Gospel by which that position is to be judged. It is the merit of this presentation to indicate, as other or larger works in the field have often failed to do, that this need for a criterion must be resolved both among pacifists and between pacifists and non-pacifists. Whether one assumes that war is compatible with the will of God or "that war is contrary to the will of God," as the World Council of Churches at Amsterdam declared, without drawing the obvious conclusions, the reasons for such a stance need definition. This book plainly takes the latter position and by giving examples of earlier reasons should deepen the apparent increasing tendency for Christian leaders and laity to do so. Some causes of that contemporary tendency are reported in the last chapter.

HENRY J. CADBURY

Haverford, Pennsylvania
September, 1971

CONTENTS

PREFACE

IF this little book helps any of its readers to become a Christian Pacifist, I shall be very glad; but this is not its primary purpose. Its original occasion was domestic; and its intent is not so much apologetic as historical. It may even have the effect of discomfiting or unsettling some readers; for the fact that Christians in other centuries thought in various ways, and that none of these ways was identical with the way in which we think to-day, is not a discovery which we make easily for ourselves or accept readily when others draw our attention to it. At the same time, the realization that differing convictions have led *some* Christians throughout the era to one and the same conclusion may dispose us to regard the conclusion as worth attention.

It is clearly impossible for a single writer to be equally well acquainted with every period in the long history of the Christian Church; and I cannot claim any special competence for more than a segment of the vast arc here described. For much of it I have depended frankly on what I believe to be the best standard text-books;[1] and in the main I have attempted no more than to pass on an impression of what I have found. The subjects on which in turn I have concentrated within each chapter are none of them meant to be either all-embracing within the period under consideration or mutually exclusive as between it and other periods. The Czech Brethren (Ch. II), for instance, certainly understood something of 'the

ministry of suffering' (Ch. III); the Quakers (Ch. IV),
equally, something of 'the means of redemption'
(Ch. V); while each new group to some extent made
its own the witness of those who had gone before.

The chapter-titles, nevertheless, have all been care-
fully chosen. It may help to prevent misunderstanding
if I illustrate what is intended from the first chapter,
'The Fear of Idolatry'. Does not the New Testament
contain other teaching which leads to a repudiation of
war? Indeed, I believe it does and hope that the book,
as it goes on, may show it does; but the fact that I see
this is not to say that the early Christians saw it too.
Was not Origen, it may be asked, aware of the humanitarian or the redemptive motive for abhorring war?
Very likely; but in so short a sketch my limited purpose is to study only organized and conscious groups
of Christian Pacifists, not isolated, prophetic figures.
I do not think that the fear of idolatry was the *only*
thing which prevented the early Christians from taking
part in war; but I do think that it was the *main* conviction underlying their attitude and the one most
characteristic of their piety as distinct from that of
later Christians. I also think it worth special attention
just because it plays a negligible part in current
Christian Pacifism and is, perhaps, the approach to
which we tend to be least sympathetic.

What is here printed was given in the form of lectures
to the annual conference of the Fellowship of Reconciliation held at St. John's College, York, during
August 1957. I desire to thank a number of people
who then kindly suggested corrections and improve-
ments. I am also sincerely grateful to the Rev. Alan
Balding, the Rev. Hampden Horne and the Rev.

Alan Knott for encouragement and assistance in the composition of the lectures; and to the officers of the Fellowship of Reconciliation for help in sponsoring publication.

It was from Alfred Neave Brayshaw (1860–1941) that I first gained my understanding of Christian Pacifism; and I shall be happy if any light cast here, or help given, may be associated with his name.

I am grateful to the World Without War Council for their desire to publish this book in a new edition. The book possesses a certain unity of sentiment, and it seems best to let the text stand, with only minimal alterations.

GEOFFREY F. NUTTALL

New College, London
Fall, 1971

1 In particular, I am indebted in Ch. III to Professor H. A. Bender's fine biography, *Conrad Grebel.* I should also like to draw attention to Dr. Peter Brock's book on *The Political and Social Doctrines of the Unity of Czech Brethren* (The Hague, 1957), with its important study of Peter Czelčický.

Christian Pacifism in History

I

THE FEAR OF IDOLATRY

MY purpose in what follows is not so much to give a straight narrative account of Christian Pacifism as to let down the plummet, as it were, and to take soundings at different periods in Christian history. This method appears to me to have a number of advantages. In the first place, to offer a straight narrative history of Christian Pacifism would hardly be possible. The story is too discontinuous, the existence, or at least the appearance, of pacifists and pacifist witness within the Church is too occasional and sporadic. At the same time, the story would take too long, and we should almost certainly become burdened with too much detail. We shall gain more and remember more if we do a good deal of limiting and selecting; and I propose that we restrict ourselves to five main periods or groups, endeavouring to see what have been the outstanding and distinguishing characteristics of each of them, without any pretensions to covering all the ground. Furthermore, if we thus concentrate on inner principles rather than on the personalities and fortunes of leading individuals—though we will not neglect these—we may hope to find something at times which can be related to our own understanding of the pacifist interpretation of the

Gospel. We can at least inquire into the continuing relevance for ourselves of the various principles which will present themselves.

I can imagine that to many it may come as a surprise that the principles which have led Christians to accept pacifism have in fact been different at different times. But so it is. The title of Professor John Ferguson's book, *The Enthronement of Love*, seems to most of us so obvious, and so adequate a summary of the first-principle which makes *us* pacifists, that we find it difficult to imagine any other. God is our Father; God loves us, all of us; His will and ways are love; war is a denial of love, and thus is contrary to His nature and will. This is sufficient for us. Need there be any other argument? Perhaps there need not be; but there certainly has been; and our minds may be usefully exercised in considering some of the other arguments. As a matter of fact, our concentration on the primacy of love in the nature of God, and therefore in the Gospel—or good news—about Him, and therefore in the social, national and international implications of the Gospel, is a relatively modern phenomenon. It is present in certain leading thinkers of earlier ages; but in general I do not find it with any prominence earlier than about a hundred years ago. We shall return to this theme in the last lecture; but you must not expect to hear much about love before then. Nevertheless, groups of Christian Pacifists have existed within the Church in earlier generations. Except, it might be argued, in the Early Church, they have been small. They have never been so many, so vocal and well organized, or (within limits) so respected as in the present century. The perception that war is an issue which must trouble the Christian conscience, whatever position be taken up with regard to it, is something new in the history of the Church. But Christian Pacifists have existed; and it is of interest, both historically and theologically, to see the various avenues they have traversed to reach their pacifist convictions.

My five titles are thus meant to indicate some of these avenues: the approaches which were made use of by the early Christians in the first three centuries; by a variety of sects in the Middle Ages; by the Swiss Anabaptists and Dutch Mennonites in the sixteenth century; by the English Quakers in the seventeenth century; and lastly our own approach in the twentieth. In each lecture I shall do what I can to suggest something of the historical circumstances and atmosphere of the time, and to offer some critical appreciation of the insights and emphases controlling pacifist convictions. To some extent I think it is true that each successive group, whether consciously or not, built on the foundations laid, or the substructure left, by those who had gone before, accepting earlier perceptions or arguments and adding something of their own; and I would hold that it is our duty to do the same.

Christianity is a distinctively historical religion. The events of history in the life and death of Jesus are of primary importance for us; and at all times we believe that God seeks to enter into our lives, and to make Himself known to us and to others, in and through those lives lived out on the plane of history, as we are sensitive to, and learn of, His leadings; and therefore we can learn through earlier generations. Christians can never say 'life began yesterday', or boast an irresponsible illiteracy. There is no infallibility given to the Church; of course, men make mistakes in every age, and we have to use our best endeavours to recognize when they were wrong, as well as when they were right; but there is good reason for a humble readiness to learn from Christians of past days, even when their ways of thinking were very different from our own.

To turn then to our first group or period, the Early Church during the first three centuries of the Christian era; and first to explain why only in the first three centuries. The age of the Early Church is generally regarded as continuing to the middle of the fifth century, when the period of defining the Christian Faith in the best terms available in the philosophical thought of the time reached its climax at the Council of Chalcedon in A.D. 451; but within those four centuries there is a point of cardinal importance, which divides them into two unequal periods. This is the year 313, when Constantine the Great, who in 307 had been proclaimed Emperor while on military service in York, and who in 311 had been converted to the Christian faith, made Christianity the official religion of the Roman Empire. As a consequence of this, everything was altered for the Christians, and has remained different ever since. 'A turning-point in European history', 'an erratic block which has diverted the stream of human history',[1] are phrases used of Constantine by Professor Norman Baynes, who, I suppose, is the greatest recent authority on him. Before Constantine, persecution of the Christians was not incessant; but they were liable to persecution at any time, they never knew when persecution might break over their heads; and it did, in fact, grow worse with every

successive outbreak, the worst persecution of all being
only two or three years before Constantine became
emperor; after him Christians have been persecuted
with great violence in some parts of the world—and I
say nothing for the moment of their persecutions of
one another—but since 313 they have never again been
liable to persecution as the official policy throughout
the civilized world. Constantine thus altered things
for good (so far as the Christian era has yet run);
and it was natural for Christians to reverence him with
honours almost divine, at least to regard him as the
equal of the apostles.

Yet it is open to argument whether it really was 'for
good', literally; whether spiritually the Church did
not lose more than it gained. For a century previously
there had been what C. J. Cadoux calls 'the gradual
and steady growth throughout the Church of a certain
moral laxity', a 'process of conformity to the ways of
the world';[2] and in a sense the battle was lost in 313:
the battle, I mean, to be in the world, yet not of it:
the battle to redeem the world, not being conformed
to the world but being transformed, so as in the power
of the Spirit to overcome the evil in the world with good.
For, when the State accepted the Church and as a
consequence the Church accepted the State, in large
measure the Church also accepted the world and the
ways of the world. Just as the bishops, whose dioceses
were often co-terminous with the areas of secular
government, became increasingly secular officers, even
becoming responsible for preserving intact the fortifica-
tion of the walls of their cities, so at the Council of
Arles which was held in 314, only one year after 313,
and which was attended by three British bishops, it

was ruled that soldiers who deserted the colours should
be excommunicated. The three bishops were all bishops
of sees which were also military towns, such as York.
It is a striking illustration of the fact that since 313
the Church has officially accepted war. As W. E.
Orchard tersely sums up the situation, 'Christianity
has accepted the State, and . . . this carries with it
the necessity for . . . the waging of war'.[3]

How far Constantine's conversion to Christianity
was sincere, and if sincere how far it went, is a question
which scholars still dispute: about his character and
policy there are several 'fatal ambiguities', as they
have been called. Some think that, when he transferred
his devotion from the sun, of which formerly he had
been a worshipper, to Jesus Christ, it was primarily
from a desire to win over and use the Church for his
secular purposes as a bulwark of unity in the Empire.
The occasion of his conversion is said to have been a
vision of the Cross athwart the sun, with the legend 'By
this conquer'; and he accordingly had the Cross
inscribed on the soldiers' standards in place of the
pagan images there previously. Later his mother,
Helen, to whom a church in York, said to be on the
site of her husband's tomb, is dedicated, sent Constantine the nails from the True Cross, which she believed
she had discovered; and what did Constantine do with
the nails? What he did was to make them 'into bridle-
bits and a helmet, which he used in his military
expeditions'.[4] In Milman's sounding phrase, 'For the
first time the meek and peaceful Jesus became a God of
battle, and the cross, the holy sign of Christian redemption, a banner of bloody strife'.[5] Before many years
were past, St. Athanasius, the great theologian to

whose inflexible stand the Church was established in the Trinitarian orthodoxy which it still holds, 'declared that it was . . . praiseworthy to kill enemies in war'; while within a century, in A.D. 416, 'non-Christians were' actually 'forbidden to serve in the army',[6] which was thus to become the preserve of the Church.

The wheel was come full circle. For while it is known that by A.D. 173 a certain legion 'contained a considerable number of Christian soldiers' and 'there is no extant indication that any disapproval of their military status was expressed by the Church of their day',[7] until then, 'apart from Cornelius and the one or two soldiers who may have been baptized with him by Peter at Caesarea and the gaoler baptized by Paul at Philippi, we have no direct or reliable evidence for the existence of a single Christian soldier';[8] and while, from that time onwards, 'there is evidence to show that . . . considerable numbers of Christians served in the imperial armies', 'the tendency to refuse service' continued to be, 'even towards the middle of the third century, still very strong in the Christian Church'.[9] One Christian, indeed, is known to have been put to death for refusing to serve as late as A.D. 298, within fifteen years of the Great Change effected by Constantine. This gradual but increasing readiness to serve in the State's armies has to be seen as part of the 'steady and serious falling-off from the high idealism of primitive times' in general, which I have mentioned already. As C. J. Cadoux expresses it, 'the acclimatization of the Christian conscience . . . to the use of the sword' was part of 'the general Christian surrender to the spirit of the world'.[10] The revolution which Constantine suddenly instituted in practice was possible only, we may say, by the gradual dissolution in principle which had preceded it.

It is easy enough for us to suppose that this was so. To look out through the eyes of the early Christians, to grasp what was in fact the principle which slowly dissolved, is more difficult. ' "The whole world lies in the power of the Evil One" ', Cadoux submits, 'is a fairly representative summary of the general Christian position': 'the world' meaning the 'heathen social system, manifesting itself in various human institutions'; and 'of these institutions, the State was at once the chief and the summary, . . . the main visible embodiment of "the world" in the bad sense'.[11] This judgement Cadoux supports with quotations from many Christian writers in one period after another. 'Of the state of the human race beyond the limits of the Christian Church, the writers of this period take on the whole a very black view' are the words in which he sums up the period A.D. 110–180; and for the next seventy years he says, 'The Christian writers of this period, like their predecessors, paint the condition of the non-Christian world around them in very black colours'.[12] Ernst Troeltsch expresses himself thus: 'the world with all its ordinances came to be regarded as a solid and unchangeable mass of evil, a system which could only be accepted or rejected *en bloc*': 'in participating in the life of the world the Christian submits to the consequences of sin'.[13] Consequently, 'Christians tended to hold themselves aloof as far as possible from the life of the world around them'. In the first century there is 'no evidence of any Christian . . . taking part in political life'; and even in the third we still have a 'profession of entire unconcern in the matter of political

ambitions and interests'.[14] 'The idea of a Christian
civilization, of a spirit which should penetrate, mould,
and renew the common life, was entirely absent.'[15]
The more perceptive minds among the pagans not
unnaturally charged Christians with enjoying the
benefits of the Empire and its peace while contributing
nothing to ensure its preservation. 'If all did as the
Christians', wrote the pagan Celsus in c. 178, 'there
would be nothing to prevent things from getting into
the hands of the barbarians': it is an argument which
Christian Pacifists still have to meet. H. M. Gwatkin
argues, indeed, that at times the persecution of the
Christians was a direct outcome of irritation at their
political aloofness: when in 256 Franks and Goths
and Berbers were all on the march and the Empire's
'frontiers were broken through on all sides', 'the great
corporations of the Christians', he says, 'even yet
maintained their selfish isolation. Not a hand would
they lift to save a sinking world'.[16]

We thus have to recognize that the early Christians'
refusal to take part in war was mainly one expression
among many of their refusal to take part in the life
of the world, or in the activity of the State, at all.
'Just because public life was wholly interwoven with
heathenism, Christians were compelled to withdraw
from it.'[17] But furthermore, just as 'the State was . . .
the main visible embodiment of "the world" in a bad
sense', so military service was the main visible embodiment of the State in a bad sense. For every soldier
had to take a military oath in rites 'over which the
heathen gods presided', involving 'a confession of
the Emperor's deity inconsistent with the place of
Christ'; and to this, as to the heathen images on the

soldiers' standards and to 'the pagan ceremonial with which so many military acts and operations were invested',[18] a devout Christian had an unconquerable objection. It was idolatry.

While in his two books, *The Early Christian Attitude to War* and *The Early Church and the World*, on which as the standard authorities I have drawn largely, C. J. Cadoux argues with some asperity that this was not the only ground for refusal of military service by the early Christians, he shows incontestably that it was the main ground. He says himself that '*except* in the matter of idolatry, Christians were on principle obedient to the commands of the State'.[19] I think that their fear of idolatry bears dwelling on, for the reason that it is a principle distinctive of their own piety rather than of that in later ages, and also because it is not a principle which lodges easily in our own minds.

We shall perhaps find less difficulty in the imaginative effort needed to appreciate the importance for the early Church of this principle—the fear of idolatry—if we remember the Jewish origin of the first Christians. With a celerity which is not altogether explainable, the Jewish Christians fade away in the history of the Church, and converts are made not, as at first, from Judaism but from the pagan world. Nevertheless the Church retained, both for good and for evil, a great deal of its Jewish heritage; and first and foremost the monotheism which was Israel's distinctive faith and the inspired scriptures, now to be called the Old Testament, in which that monotheistic faith was recorded and enjoined. Now few things, I suppose, were, or are, so engrained in Judaism, so burnt into the Jewish soul, as the fear of idolatry. 'Thou shalt have no other gods but me.' Israel's supreme religious duty, her prime contribution to the world, was this faith in Yahweh, the one God, before whom all other gods were idols. Consequently, every mildest approach to anything remotely resembling idolatry was abominable, and to be avoided even at the cost of life itself.

The story of Israel's stand over against Rome is, in fact, a heroic one. Israel insisted on, and won, privileges from Rome which were granted to no other subject people. 'The imperial currency circulated in Judaea', as we know from the denarius which Jesus handled; but 'for the use of the strict Jews who would not touch a coin bearing the Emperor's superscription', 'money was coined' by imperial permission, which 'bore no image'.[20] Again, 'The Emperor could get all the soldiers he needed by voluntary enlistment' . . . so that 'any attempt to force a man into the ranks . . . was a very rare occurrence';[21] but to avoid offending Jewish susceptibilities, 'every Jew was exempt from military service'. Once more, there was 'a handful of Roman soldiers in Jerusalem'; but they were 'ordered to leave their standards' (with the hateful pagan emblems) 'at Caesarea',[22] the civil capital; and when Pontius Pilate, despite the order, sent troops to Jerusalem *with* their standards, the Jews at once petitioned him against it with vehemence. He surrounded them with soldiers; but they protested that they would die rather than submit; and Pilate yielded.

This is the background of early Christian refusal to serve in the imperial armies. The Church began as a Jewish sect; and for some years this fact provided it with a measure of protection from persecution; for the Government was blind to any significant difference and permitted the Christians to enjoy the tolerance and privileges already granted to the Jews. It was not long, as I have remarked, before the Church ceased effectually to make converts from the Jews, who quite soon, in fact, often fanned the persecution of Christians; it was none the less natural that the Church should continue to expect the exemption from military service granted to the Jews; and that, where this was not allowed, they should plead the Jewish ground for exemption, the fear of idolatry. That this fear could still trouble the minds of Christians who later found themselves serving in the imperial armies appears from the confession of the centurion who was martyred in A.D. 298: 'If . . . those who render military service must be compelled to sacrifice to gods and emperors, then I cast down my vine-staff and belt, I renounce the standards, and I refuse to serve as a soldier'.[23]

If I may put it provocatively, the early Christian attitude to war was more like that of the people who call themselves Jehovah's Witnesses than it is comfortable for us to suppose. They 'contracted out' of all political responsibilities, as we call it to-day. 'Come ye out from among them, and touch no unclean thing': the words are to be found in the New Testament as well as in the Old. 'I would not that ye should have fellowship with devils.' 'Little children, keep yourselves from idols.' These are not popular texts to-day. 'I sat where he sat' is the text for the modern temper; or, 'Jesus, when he came out, saw much people, and was moved with compassion toward them, because they were as sheep not having a shepherd'. We are ready to proclaim the centrality of compassion and reconciliation and how 'God so loved the world'. 'Love not the world'—the prophet's text, as we may call it—we leave alone. We must be true to our own understanding of what is cardinal to the Gospel; but it would be difficult to deny that the Church is called out of the world: called out, it is true, that, back in the world, it may be the means of the world's redemption, but still called out first, to become, and in a sense perpetually to remain, different from the world, different from what the world, in its un-Christian state, can ever be. It would also be foolish to overlook the subtle winning upon men's spirits—and Christians remain men, even when they have become new men in Christ—which the world exerts so powerfully, ever drawing us, in thought and behaviour, to 'revert to type', to the worldly unredeemed type of humanity.

Worship of the Emperor, *Führer* or State, which is idolatry, has been seen to be by no means dead in this century in countries other than our own; and in our own it was perilously easy for the requirements of the State to become an idol during wartime. We cannot always have a William Temple at York or Canterbury to proclaim from on high that we are Christians first, and Englishmen second. Perhaps just because of his great gifts and versatility, Temple was keenly aware of the continuing temptation to idolatry, and of the variety of idols that would keep us from a following Christ which is unreserved. We shall not be effectual in pointing to the idolatry of the State and its safety, if, for instance, we are patently idolizing ourselves and our own comfort and security: 'one thing thou lackest'. But as pacifists we have a peculiar duty to be sensitive to, and to warn others of, the particular idolatry to which the nature of the State makes it inclined, even when there is no open nationalism, jingoism or totalitarianism. No government can rightly claim implicit, uncritical trust, what Hitler called *blinde Treue,* as the Bishop of Manchester once forcefully reminded us. We are no longer antipathetic to government as such. This raises problems more acute than most of us, I fancy, are inclined to face; but at least we may say that we work always with a basis of judgement which has a different reference from the secular sanctions of any earthly government. We have to be always ready for the conflict to arise, 'We must obey God rather than men'; and then to throw open our windows towards Jerusalem.

NOTES

[1] N. H. Baynes, *Constantine the Great and the Christian Church,* p. 3.

[2] C. J. Cadoux, *The Early Church and the World,* p. 279.

[3] W. E. Orchard, introd. to C. J. Cadoux, *The Early Christian Attitude to War.*

[4] *E.C.A.W.,* p. 256.

[5] H. H. Milman, *History of Christianity,* ii. 287.

[6] *E.C.A.W.,* p. 257.

[7] *E.C.W.,* pp. 277 f.

[8] *E.C.A.W.,* p. 97.

[9] *E.C.W.,* pp. 417, 438 f.

[10] *ibid.,* pp. 613, 615.

[11] *ibid.,* p. 166.

[12] *ibid.,* pp. 208, 293.

[13] E. Troeltsch, *The Social Teaching of the Christian Churches,* E.T., i. 101, 126.

[14] *E.C.W.,* pp. 231, 174, 534.

[15] *S.T.C.C.,* i. 126.

[16] H. M. Gwatkin, *Early Church History,* ii. 267 f.

[17] *E.C.W.,* p. 174, n. 4.

[18] *E.C.A.W.,* pp. 114 f., with n. 2.

[19] *E.C.W.,* p. 257.

[20] Wells and Barrow, *A Short History of the Roman Empire,* p. 39.

[21] *E.C.A.W.,* p. 17.

[22] Wells and Barrow, *ibid.*

[23] *E.C.A.W.,* p. 152.

II

THE LAW OF CHRIST

THE passage which we are now to make from the Early Church to the Middle Ages, especially since in effect it is from the beginnings of the Early Church to near the end of the Middle Ages, is, of course, an enormous leap: a leap of a thousand years and more. John Wycliffe died in 1384. The date of his birth is not known; but it will have been rather more than a thousand years after 313, the year when under Constantine the State accepted the Church and the Church the State; and from 1384 to this present year of 1970 is less than 600 years.

Not that in the period we are now to study men were aware, as we are, of the immense change which had come over the face of things. In words of the historian Bryce which deserve to be famous if they are not: 'through all that period which we call the Dark and Middle Ages, men's minds were possessed by the belief that all things continued as they were from the beginning, that no chasm never to be recrossed lay between them and that ancient world to which they had not ceased to look back. We who are centuries removed can see that there had passed a great and wonderful change upon thought, and art, and literature, and politics, and society itself: . . . But so gradual was the change that each generation felt it passing over them no more than a man feels that perpetual transformation by which his body is renewed from year to year; . . . There is nothing more modern than the critical spirit which fastens upon the differences between the minds of men in one age and in another; which endeavours to make each age its own interpreter, and judge what it did or produced by a relative standard.'[1]

By way of introduction to this lecture I want to quote a further short passage from Bryce's great book, *The Holy Roman Empire*, one of the few books first published so long ago as 1864 which are still standard authorities on their subject. 'He who begins to read the history of the Middle Ages', Bryce writes, 'is alternately amused and provoked by the seeming absurdities that meet him at every step. He finds writers proclaiming amidst universal assent magnificent theories which no one attempts to carry out. He sees men stained with every vice full of sincere devotion to a religion which, even when its doctrines were most obscured, never sullied the purity of its moral teaching. . . . Men's impulses were more violent and their conduct more reckless than is usually seen in modern communities; while the absence of a criticizing and measuring spirit made them surrender their minds more unreservedly than they would now do to a complete and imposing theory'. 'At no time in the world's history', he continues, 'has theory, professing all the while to control practice, been so utterly divorced from it. Ferocious and sensual, that age worshipped humility and asceticism: there has never been a purer ideal of love, nor a grosser profligacy of life'.[2]

These passages set the background against which the groups whom we are now to consider were reacting,

indeed rebelling: the few—and they are few in any
age—who were offended by the gulf between theory and
practice, ideal and realization, until they came themselves to hold a different theory and to plead an ideal
quite other. The accepted ideal of the Middle Ages
was that of the *mundus Christianus*, the Christian world.
The old disparity, the old enmity, between the world
and the Church had been forgotten. Christianity had
spread widely, and within the broad compass of Europe
there had appeared, at least in theory and intention,
that 'Christian civilization', the idea of which we
noted as so strikingly absent from the minds of the
early Christians. The old Roman Empire, which the
first Christians had known as a heathen persecuting
power, had now been transformed by the power of
Christ, it was believed, into the Holy Roman Empire,
in which the Emperor was a Christian Emperor and
the Pope an imperial Bishop: two powers equally
ordained of God, however their interrelation might be
disputed, with their different spheres included in
the working out together by similar methods of a
common purpose. Nothing, nothing whatever, lay
beyond their purview and proper control; any opposition, any criticism almost, seemed impossible, and
when made was very quickly driven underground.

'*Pax*, mot magique pour une âme médiévale',
observes M. Gilson in his study of *L'Esprit de la Philosophie Médiévale*;[3] 'we know how constantly' the word
pace is 'upon Dante's lips in the *Divina Commedia*', says
a leading Dante scholar;[4] 'we catch the thrill of
poignant longing', writes Professor Burnaby, 'which
the very word *pax*, as' St. Augustine 'spoke it, would
always stir in his hearers'.[5] It is an example of the

paradox to which Bryce calls attention that equally
in the Middle Ages the practice of war against her
enemies without, and of persecution against her
enemies within, had been sanctioned by the Church for
so many centuries that both were taken for granted; and
also that this approval both of the waging of war and
of the taking of repressive measures against heretics
and schismatics may be traced to the same St. Augustine
who so longed for peace; his yielding to this 'fatal
principle' Dr. Kidd calls 'a step not less disastrous
in the after-history of the Church than the conversion
of Constantine'.[6] Milman can even use the phrase,
'the military Christianity of the Middle Ages'.[7] 'The
Crusades had made the Pope not merely the spiritual,
but in some sort the military suzerain of Europe;
he had the power of summoning all Christendom to
his banner; the raising the Cross, the standard of the
Pope, was throughout Europe a general and compul-
sory levy' on 'all who could follow an army'.[8] Military
orders, such as those of the Knights Templars and
Hospitallers, had their place beside the monastic
and mendicant orders, such as the Benedictines and
Franciscans, in the devotion of the time.

In such a Christianity, highly organized, powerful
and all-embracing, it was possible for the voice of
Christian Pacifism to be heard but rarely, among the
few who possessed both the originality to conceive, and
then the courage to express, criticisms of the system as
a whole. It is sufficiently remarkable that criticisms
were made or heard at all. Yet through all the high
grandeur of the mediæval centuries, critics both of
current theory or doctrine and of current practice
persisted. Their repudiation of war, when they did

repudiate it, is like that of the early Christians in being
but part of a wider reaction. Only now, instead of
being rebels against a heathen empire, the heretics
were rebels against a worldly and secularized Church;
and in some ways their case was worse than that of
the early Christians. No longer could they claim—no
doubt they did claim it, but only in defiance of the
facts—that their position was clearly the only possible
position open to true Christians. They were now a
sect, in separation from, in opposition to, the official
Church. The fellowship was broken. Their pacifist
convictions had therefore to spring from a fresh source.
Idolatry pure and simple, military service could now
hardly be called. In a deeper sense it might still be so,
but there were no longer heathen rites to be performed
or heathen emperor or deity to whom allegiance
must be sworn and sacrifice made. They had to find
a new foundation principle. They did so by returning
to and recovering the Bible, which by the contemporary
Church was forbidden to the hands and eyes of laymen, and the interpretation of which was reserved
for the priests as the Church's official and informed
teachers.

Upon these mediæval heretics much work has been
done. Their repudiation of war is generally treated as
a side-issue. They have been studied mainly because
of their repudiation of the mediæval doctrine of the
ministry and sacraments, indeed of all that was
included in the conception of priesthood. Protestant
writers have welcomed them as precursors of the
Reformation. Interest in them has weakened, however, with the decrease in the abhorrence of Rome
and with the recovery of 'the Church' as an ideal

concept, which are two of many silent effects of the Oxford Movement. One twentieth-century writer, Ernst Troeltsch, *has* made a serious effort to assess the significance of the sect-type, as he calls it, in distinction from the church-type in Christian history. His appreciation of it as what he calls 'an independent sociological type of Christian thought' has not, perhaps, won very general assent, but is worth our noting. Troeltsch quotes with approval a definition of the sect as 'the empirical representation of a community of nothing but awakened Christians, living apart from the world', and says it can 'often present in a very direct and characteristic way the essential fundamental ideas of Christianity'. 'The sect', he argues, 'appeals to the ever new common performance of the moral demands, which, at bottom, are founded only upon the Law and the Example of Christ'. 'They look upon the New Testament as the Law of God'; they 'take the Sermon on the Mount as their ideal', and 'the bond of fellowship is solely the "Law of Jesus", literally understood'.[9] These are certainly the marks of the three main heretical groups which repudiated war in the Middle Ages, namely the Waldenses of France and Northern Italy, the Lollards of this country and the Bohemian or Moravian Brethren of Bohemia, the modern Czechoslovakia.

The Waldenses take their name from a merchant of Lyons, Peter Waldo, who in 1170 sold his goods and gave them to the poor and, without seeking theological training or commissioning through ordination, went forth as an itinerant to preach the gospel of poverty. Amid the wealth of the mediæval Church poverty exercised a powerful appeal as an ideal, and is found on the lips of many sensitive souls, among them St. Francis, who some thirty-six years later in his turn sold his goods for a life of poverty. Some scholars in fact argue a direct influence of Waldo on Francis; and to us it is of interest to observe that Francis' Tertiaries, or Third Order of laypeople, 'were at first forbidden to bear arms';[10] though this is, perhaps, no more than an extension of the rule of the Church that *clergy* should not bear arms (a rule which in practice was not obeyed).[11] What disturbed the authorities about Waldo was not his preaching of poverty but (as later with Wesley) his irregular preaching, his disobedience. 'St. Francis knew how to obey and . . . Waldo did not.'[12] Francis sought and gained papal sanction for his enterprise and remained within the fold of the Church; Waldo was excommunicated, and his followers became a sect which in 1215 was formally condemned. Their history since that date has been, and still is (for there is still a Waldensian Church in Northern Italy), a bitter tale of virulent persecution; and no doubt the persecution helped them, as it helped the early Christians, to repudiate war.

Their essential ground for doing so, however, was that they believed it to be forbidden in Scripture. 'In the return to Scripture', it has been said, 'we find the actual beginning of the Waldensian movement. Of no other heretics are we informed that they demanded the knowledge of Scripture and themselves distributed Scripture with such eagerness as did the Waldenses';[13] 'the Waldenses made Bible translations one of the main planks of their programme'.[14] Much traditional Christian doctrine, especially that concerning the next world, they did not attack; their interest in it was mainly as it affected practice in this world. 'With the Waldenses', says Harnack, 'the conception of the Law of Christ, as it is described in the Scriptures, stands out above all other marks by which the Church may be recognized'; 'this law is present quintessentially', he adds 'in the Sermon on the Mount'; and 'it was from the Sermon on the Mount that to them, as to so many mediæval sects, came the repudiation of oaths, military service, capital punishment and all shedding of blood'.[15]

That Peter Waldo or the Waldenses directly influenced John Wycliffe is unlikely, but the principles adopted by the two men show marked similarities. Wycliffe's personal position was not at all the same as Waldo's. While Waldo was a layman, Wycliffe was in orders and a distinguished scholar: in 1361 he was Master of Balliol College, Oxford. Nor, despite the fact that as a systematic thinker he was far more revolutionary than Waldo, did he suffer personal condemnation (let alone the martyrdom) which was the lot of many of his followers. He was like Waldo, however, in urging the translation of the Bible with which his name is now chiefly associated, and in sending out 'poor priests', as they were called, as itinerant preachers of the gospel without any episcopal licence. A link with the friars also appears again, for the friars went 'far in their support of Wycliffe before his open breach with the papacy'.[16]

In Wycliffe, as in Waldo, is exhibited 'the endeavour to set up the Bible as the sole authority and the source of the Divine law'. 'The Bible and Christianity', again, 'are everywhere designated the "Law of God" by Wyclif': his writings ring the changes on 'the law of the Lord', 'the law of Christ', 'the law of Scripture', 'the Christian law', 'the evangelical law' or 'law of the gospel'.[17] 'Christ's law is best and enough', he says, 'and other laws men should not take';[18] and 'the law of Christ in suffering injuries comes nearer to the ideal state of nature than the civil law'.[19] That his repudiation of war sprang directly from the Sermon on the Mount appears clearly in the following passage on the Lord's Prayer: 'Men that lyven in werre ben unable to have ther axinge: but thei axen ther owne dampnynge in ye fifte petitioun, for ther thei axen that God forgyve hem ther dettis that thei owen to hym, ryght as thei forgyven men that ben dettours to them. . . . And so in this fifte axinge thes men that werren now-a-daies . . . is noo good praier, but more axinge of Goddis venjaunce'.[20]

While 'strongly opposed to war',[21] Wycliffe did not in fact unreservedly condemn either war or persecution;[22] but in general, to use words of J. N. Figgis, he repudiated 'the conception of the Church as a coercive organization, and in so doing shattered the ideal which ruled men's minds from the time of St. Augustine';[23] and after his death his followers 'were determined opponents of war'.[24] 'Jesus Christ, duke of oure batel', said Nicholas of Hereford, their chief leader, 'taught us lawe of pacience, and not to fight bodily';[25] and of the 'Twelve Conclusions', which in 1395 the Lollards presented to Parliament, the tenth was a condemnation of war. A peculiar interest attaches to it as the first pacifist petition laid before the House of Commons: 'The tende conclusiun is, that manslaute be batayle . . . with outen special revelaciun is expres contrarious to the newe testament, the qwiche is a lawe of grace and ful of mercy. This conclusiun is opinly prouid be exsample of Cristis preching here in erthe, the qwiche most taute for to love and to have mercy on his enemys, and nout for to slen hem. . . . The lawe of mercy, that is the new testament, forbad al mannisslaute: . . . be mekenesse and suffraunce our beleve was multiplied, and fythteres and mansleeris Ihesu Crist hatith. . . .'[26]

There is to-day no continuing Lollard church; but the influence of Wycliffe and his followers was strong and permanent, both in this country and abroad. That the Lollards could find leaders to present their Conclusions to Parliament is evidence that in 1395 they were a force to be reckoned with; but the arch-bishop of Canterbury, Thomas Arundel, made it 'the great business of his later life . . . to resist the tide of Lollardy'.[27] In 1399 a law was passed for the burning of heretics, and two years later a tailor named William Sawtre became the first of a long line to go to the stake. Within a generation Lollardy was forced underground, nor did it ever produce another leader of the calibre of Wycliffe or even Hereford. It per-sisted, nevertheless, right up to the beginnings of the Reformation a century later, when its heresy became merged with that of the new Lutheranism. 'As late as 1521, the Bishop of London arrested nearly 500 Lollards' and 'most of the English Reformers were acquainted with Wycliffe's works'.[28] The study of unpublished episcopal registers provides increasing evidence for the continuance of the movement in many parts of the country; and it is significant that through-out the fifteenth century Lollards are found in relative strength in places which later became noted strong-holds of the Independents, Baptists and Quakers. This

is the case not only in towns such as Bristol and
Northampton, but in country places such as Amersham
and Chesham in Buckinghamshire, the district round
Almeley in Herefordshire, and parts of Montgomery-
shire.

More remarkable is the influence which Wycliffe
and the movement he initiated had on religion in
Central Europe. Associations between England and
Bohemia were then close through the fact that
Richard II's Queen, Anne, came from that country,
and 'it was the Bohemians in her train who first in-
troduced' Wycliffe's 'writings to John Huss'.[29] Visits
and correspondence between the two countries became
frequent. Lollard writings were burned by the Arch-
bishop of Prague, but Huss continued to defend them
at the University there, and wrote expressing gratitude
for the great benefits Bohemia had received from
blessed England;[30] and to-day 'many of' Wycliffe's
'writings exist in manuscript at Vienna and at Prague,
of which copies are rare or not to be found in England.'[31]
The leader of the Czech reformers, John Huss, was
'dependent on Wycliffe throughout in his thinking
and teaching'; in fact, 'the Hussite movement was
based entirely upon Wyclif's theories'.[33] Huss himself
was far more conservative than Wycliffe;[34] but when
in 1415 he was burnt at the stake at Constance, the
fires which in England had only smouldered burst into
a flame so fierce that they eventually 'involved the
revolt of the Bohemian nation'.[35]

The Lollard emphasis upon 'the Law of God' was
preserved; but doubtless because of the political and
nationalist element caught up into the Czech movement, its radical members were so untrue to the pacifist

tendency of Wycliffe's teaching that they were driven
into armed revolution, their purpose being that 'the
Law of God' should be 'imposed upon the life of
Society . . . by a community of Christian warriors for
God'.[36] For years there was terrible bloodshed, till in
1453 the fortified hill called Tábor, from which as
their headquarters they were named Taborites, was
finally destroyed. From the ruins of their hopes arose
a purified community (much as two centuries later the
Quakers arose out of the ashes of the Civil Wars in this
country), which rejected all ways of violence. The
movement's inspirer, a layman named Peter Czelčický
(c. 1390–c. 1460), may have been a soldier as a young
man;[37] but 'as early as 1420' he had asserted that 'the
force of arms was altogether inadmissible in matters of
religion', and eventually he came to hold that 'war
under any circumstances was an accursed practice'.[38]
'As he took the Sermon on the Mount as his guide', says
a standard historian of the movement, 'he made it the
law for every detail of life'.[39] Peter was 'familiar
with the writings of Wycliffe'[40] but 'refused to have
anything to do with any Wycliffite propaganda which
was supported by violence'.[41] The Moravian Church,
as the movement which he initiated is now generally
known, was also in touch from its beginnings with the
Waldenses, union with whom it at one time thought
possible. In the year 1957 it celebrated its quincen-
tenary; for it was in 1457 that it became an organized
group with the title, 'The Brethren of the Law of
Christ'.[42] The Brethren then resolved that they would
not defend themselves by force of arms.[43] The movement is described by Karl Holl as 'the first great attempt
of the lay world to realize a religious life which was not

based upon a compromise with the world, a life which would not be content with formal consecrations and a semi-morality, but one which took the whole of life under its wing'.[44] 'After the Christian civilization of the Church had proved itself to be a secularization, . . .' says Ernst Troeltsch, 'and the attempt to realize the . . . Law . . . of God by violence had proved itself to be a bloody Utopia', 'this is a complete return to the social ideal of the Early Church'.[45]

The outstanding characteristic of these mediæval pacifists, as at the outset we observed to be true generally of the sect-movement in which they take their place, is their return to the Bible; within the Bible to the New Testament; and within the New Testament to the Sermon on the Mount. The Reformation also is marked by a return to the Bible, but by a return to the Bible as a whole; in some things to the Old Testament more than to the New; and within the New Testament to the Epistles certainly more than to the Gospels. It is only within the last hundred years that the Gospels have been so prominent in study and in devotion as they are to-day. It may be that this has contributed to the present increased openness among Christians to pacifist conviction.

As we look back to an age when it was forbidden and highly dangerous to possess a copy of the Bible, we cannot but admire the heretics who insisted on its authority and who pointed men to the purity of the Gospels over against the compromises and corruptions of contemporary Christianity; and if, with a certain simplicity of approach laymen fastened upon the Sermon on the Mount as providing them with the directions for living which they sought, there is in this nothing very surprising. But why, you may ask, did they so regularly call the Sermon on the Mount, and indeed the biblical revelation of God as a whole, 'the Law of Christ'? Was there not involved in their doing so a certain narrowing down of Christianity to rules and regulations, reflecting and probably also producing a legalism of spirit in themselves? I think there was; but they were men of their time. In his book on *The English Clergy . . . in the Later Middle Ages*, Hamilton Thompson speaks of 'the prevailing spirit of legalism'.[46] 'In the intellectual world of the Middle Ages', as Troeltsch puts it, 'the conception of law was a fundamental constituent element, and . . . every new formulation always leads anew to the Law of Jesus.'[47]

To-day we are perhaps too ready to overlook the continuing element of law, and indeed of justice, within the Gospel. After all, justice is very much better than injustice; and a belief in it is, often, the first step towards a truly Christian relationship. God is not unjust, or less than just. The point of the parable of the labourers is not the condemnation of a belief in justice: justice is satisfied. What is condemned is envy: 'Didst thou not agree with me for a penny? Take that thine is, and go thy way'. 'Is thine eye evil because I am good?': what is condemned is jealousy, as again in the reply to the Prodigal's elder brother: 'Son, all that I have is thine', it's so unworthy to be a dog in the manger, you could have had a kid any time for the asking. We have to get beyond justice, certainly; as to love mercy is beyond doing justly; but we get beyond it only by getting through it, not over it or by by-passing it. There is a wise word of George Fox to the Ranters that they 'start up to be as Gods; and

never came through the Prophets, nor Moses house'.[48]
'What did Moses command you?' Jesus will ask.
'What is written in the law? How readest thou?' 'If
thou wilt enter into life, keep the commandments.'
Jesus did not abrogate the Ten Commandments. In His
reply to the rich young man He repeats their authority;
and in the Sermon on the Mount He in one sense adds
to their comprehensiveness.

Yet in another sense He goes altogether beyond
them: the principle of the extra, of the second mile, is
not a legal principle at all. The bearing of one another's
burdens, which is what Paul calls 'the law of Christ',
is hardly patient of legal enforcement. It is nearer to
what elsewhere he calls 'the law of the Spirit of Life'.
This vital, free, spontaneous element the mediæval
pacifists seem to have missed; so might we have done,
had we been independent lay searchers under bitter
persecution in a world which had not yet received the
new notes of self-giving grace and suffering love which
came in with the Reformation. We cannot mistake a
certain hardness about them, especially about Wycliffe,
the most originating mind among them all. 'So far as
can be judged', writes J. N. Figgis, 'he had no literary
or artistic sense at all'; 'he is without historical sentiment'; 'there is no strain of mysticism in his writings'.[49]
More recently Dom David Knowles has observed 'the
impersonal manner that distinguishes all' Wycliffe's
'writing and that seems to reflect a mind to which
personal affection was a stranger': 'in the realm of
mere abuse he helped to found a genre of English
writing', Professor Knowles adds; his 'hatred could
be satisfied only with the complete extinction of his
opponent'.[50] One is reminded of a phrase about

George Fox, 'admitting no weapon but the tongue, he used that unsparingly'.[51] Pacifists remain human and are thus often inconsistent. We shall be wise if we learn from Wycliffe and the mediæval heretics the dangers of the one-track mind and of the legalism of spirit which is congenial to it. Yet our debt to them is far, far greater than this. For we find ourselves 'confronted' we would say, in a Quaker phrase, 'with a Christianity, the Christianity of the Gospels, that calls for a radical transformation of man, for the creation of a new type of person and for the building of a new social order, and' we 'take this with utmost seriousness as a thing to be ventured and tried'.[52] And for such an approach, this endeavour after *applied* Christianity, the mediæval heretics, with their appeal to 'the Law of Christ', however incomplete their understanding of it, were the pioneers, the often suffering and sometimes martyred pioneers.

NOTES

[1] J. Bryce, *The Holy Roman Empire*, p. 271.
[2] *ibid.*, pp. 130, 118.
[3] E. Gilson, *L'Esprit de la Philosophie Médiévale*, 2me. série, p. 67.
[4] E. G. Gardner, *Proc. Brit. Acad.*, X. 109.
[5] J. Burnaby, *Amor Dei*, p. 53.
[6] B. J. Kidd, *A History of the Church to A.D. 461*, iii. 17 f.
[7] H. H. Milman, *History of Christianity*, ii. 288.
[8] *id.*, *History of Latin Christianity*, v. 172.
[9] Ernst Troeltsch, *op. cit.*, i. 338, 434, 334, 336 f., 332, 357.
[10] C. J. Cadoux, *Catholicism and Christianity*, p. 621.
[11] *ibid.*, p. 622.
[12] A. L. Maycock, *The Inquisition*, p. 36.
[13] Johann Martinů, *Die Waldesier u. die husitische Reformation in Böhmen*, p. 58, citing Herzog.
[14] S. Runciman, *The Medieval Manichee*, p. 168.
[15] A. Harnack, *Lehrbuch d. Dogmensgeschichte*, 3rd edn., pp. 429, 435, 384, n. 2.
[16] Aubrey Gwynn, *The English Austin Friars in the Time of Wyclif*, p. 249.

[17] E. Troeltsch, i. 437.

[18] *Wyclif: Select English Writings*, ed. H. B. Workman, p. 6.

[19] E. Troeltsch, i. 437.

[20] H. B. Workman, p. 114.

[21] *ibid.*, p. xxiii.

[22] J. N. Figgis, in *Typical English Churchmen*, 2nd ser., p. 31.

[23] *ibid.*

[24] H. B. Workman, p. 113.

[25] *ibid.*

[26] *Eng. Hist. Rev.*, xxii. 302.

[27] *D.N.B.*, *s.v.* Arundel.

[28] A. F. Pollard, *Thomas Cranmer*, p. 91.

[29] *D.N.B.*, *s.v.* Anne of Bohemia.

[30] J. T. Müller, *Geschichte d. Böhmischen Brüder*, pp. 6 f.

[31] *D.N.B.*, *s.v.* Anne of Bohemia.

[32] J. T. Müller, p. 11.

[33] E. Troeltsch, i. 362.

[34] J. T. Müller, p. 11.

[35] Bartlet & Carlyle, *Christianity in History*, p. 477.

[36] E. Troeltsch, i. 364.

[37] J. E. Hutton, *Short History of the Moravian Church*, p. 14. The first extended account of Peter Czelčický published in English appeared in 1957 as chapter I in Peter Brock, *The Political and Social Doctrines of the Unity of Czech Brethren in the Fifteenth and Early Sixteenth Centuries* (Mouton, 's-Gravenhage).

[38] D. Benham, *Notes on the Origin and Episcopate of the Bohemian Brethren*, pp. 22, 24.

[39] J. E. Hutton, p. 15.

[40] E. Langton, *History of the Moravian Church*, p. 28.

[41] E. Troeltsch, i. 367.

[42] E. Langton, p. 30.

[43] *ibid.*

[44] E. Troeltsch, i. 366 f.

[45] *ibid.*

[46] A. H. Thompson, *op. cit.*, p. 6.

[47] E. Troeltsch, i. 433.

[48] G. Fox and J. Nayler, *A Word from the Lord, Unto . . . the World* (1654), p. 13.

[49] J. N. Figgis, *op. cit.*, pp. 33, 12, 41.

[50] David Knowles, *The Religious Orders in England*, ii. 101 f., 104.

[51] *D.N.B.*, *s.v.* Fox.

[52] *Friends and War* (1928), reprint of 1920 All Friends Conference statement, p. 14.

III

THE MINISTRY OF SUFFERING

WE can none of us ever be too thankful for the Reformation. Even if we are Roman Catholics, we still have cause for thankfulness, however mingled it must then be with sorrow; for the movement within the Roman Catholic Church evoked by the Reformation, which as a consequence became known as the Counter-Reformation, was a movement of purification from which the Church itself emerged reformed, though by no means Protestant. But within the Roman Church pacifist convictions are still frowned upon by authority; it is almost entirely within the Protestant communions that the pacifist movement has appeared and grown, at least in any organized and effective fashion. We may regret that of the several Protestant Churches so few have committed themselves officially to the pacifist interpretation of the Gospel; but they do now generally recognize it as a tenable position, even if very much of a minority issue; and for that we may be thankful.

But indeed we must be thankful for very much more. The Reformation was a movement of great complexity, in which much that was mistaken, questionable or even evil was mingled with idealism, devotion and achievement: intellectual, political, social, economic considerations played their part alongside more purely religious motives. In some ways it was more like a revolution than what is generally meant by a reformation. When great numbers of people are swayed, even by appeals which are primarily religious in their intent, there is likely to be in the result a degree of impurity of which one would properly be critical in a religious leader. I say this, because within the sphere of our particular interest the Reformation came such a very little way. It is disappointing, and you may well ask why. Why do I, nevertheless, speak of the Reformation under such a sense of debt?

I suppose that the two outstanding things which, as Protestants, and religiously speaking, we owe to the Reformation are what is called 'the open Bible', and what from different points of view is called 'justification by faith', 'the priesthood of all believers' or 'the right of private judgement'. In other words, the Reformers aimed to bring the Bible to the homes and the hearts of the people, translated into their own languages, so that all their belief might rest no longer upon the authority of the Church, in the sense of the institution with which they were familiar, but upon the authority of the Bible; and one effect of everyman's being encouraged to go to the Bible for himself was an assurance, which they also found confirmed *in* the Bible, that everyman might know God for himself: not by himself but for himself, as God's Spirit within him answered to the truths which, together with other Christians, he was seeking, and finding, in the Bible. There is thus a wonderful sense of liberation about the Reformation; as also, for us who in the previous lecture sought to enter a little into the longings and struggle of the mediæval sects, a great sense of achievement and triumph. The Bible, the secret possession even of parts of which had been their greatest joy, 'as deliteful as her lijf', as the Lollards said (and sometimes it cost them their life), was now brought out into the open. In this country a copy of it, together with Erasmus' *Paraphrases* explaining it, also translated into English, was set up in every parish church by Act of Parliament. I say again, you may well ask: why was it then that the Reformers, and the Protestant Churches which rose out of their labours, did not find in the Bible the message of pacifism, as Waldo and Wycliffe and Czelčický had done, and as we do?

Mainly, I think, for two reasons: one that was bound up with the nature of the Reformation as a whole; and one that was more a matter of unhappy circumstance. In the first place, the Reformers' desire was to convert, to bring over, whole communities of people: their city, their state, their nation; and it was a time when nationalism was kindling fiercely. The Reformers could not be content to convert merely their friends or a few already like-minded persons. They were too big for that. The truth they saw they saw as for everyone. Moreover, it was not a time of doubt or hesitation: they inherited the assurance, the certainty, the infallibility claimed by the Roman Church and her priests. But sacerdotalism they were engaged in throwing off; and they could hardly hope to do it successfully, it seemed, unless they engaged in their support the only other comparable authority available to them, that of the State, for which, surely, as in the days of Israel of old, God had a high place in His purpose for the world. Over against Rome, therefore, they looked to the strong arm of the sovereign, whether of a monarch, to be a 'godly Prince' as in Germany or a 'Supreme Head' or 'Supreme Governor' as in this country, or of a City

Council as in democratic Switzerland. For both evangelistic and defensive reasons, therefore, the State, the Government, was involved in the Reformation from the beginning, in a way it had not been in the Waldensian, Lollard and Brethren's movements in the Middle Ages; and pacifism was no more likely to appeal to a Government in the sixteenth century than in our own. Men did not then fear Communist Russia; but attack by the Turk was no idle or infrequent fear.

At the same time, the Reformation and what it promised proved headily exhilarating for the common people, who are never inclined to act with the measured restraint of their more educated leaders. In certain quarters the movement quickly got out of hand. The Bohemian Wars waged in fury by the Taborites were still a living and fearsome memory; and when in 1524–5 the Peasants in Germany rose in revolt, with encouragement from men who had come under Luther's influence, Luther was prompt in dissociating himself from it. Surely it was wise to call in the secular arm to quell what might bring down his cause in its own ruins. Ten years later there was another, more localized but even more terrifying, disaster at Münster, where a party of Anabaptists, seized by an apocalyptic and militant spirit similar to that which had possessed the Bohemian Taborites, went to un-heard-of lengths in holy slaughter, with 'an excess of fanaticism which shocked the civilized world'.[1] The Anabaptist cause was put out of court for at least a century; and, since the only organized Reformation groups to stand for pacifism were Anabaptist, the cause of pacifism was put out of court also. That

acts of violence should preclude the acceptance of
the principles of peace is paradoxical; but action and
reaction in history is often not logical; and, just as
after the Peasants' Revolt Luther retreated in alarm
into a reliance upon the secular arm which was gravely
to colour his whole outlook (as indeed also the outlook
of Lutheranism ever since), so after Münster men took
it for granted that any man preaching believers'
baptism must be dangerous and were unable to hear
those who in fact preached peace and suffering love.

I say Luther 'retreated', because 'in his earlier
period', as Troeltsch remarks, 'Luther's outlook was
often very similar to that of the sect-type'.[2] 'At the
outset of his career Luther had reckoned on the
influence of smaller groups of' those whom he called
'earnest Christians to leaven . . . the general compul-
sory religion of the Territorial Church'[3]: he 'thought
of entering' their 'names . . . in a special book and
having them meet separately from the mass of nominal
Christians'.[4] There is indeed a simplicity and a direct-
ness about the early Luther, to which leaders of the
later sect-movements did not hesitate to appeal; there
are even passages in his writings to which some pointed
as evidence of his 'original rejection of war'.[5] Whatever impulses in this direction he may have had were,
however, soon overlaid and 'in the uniform Territorial
Church' which was the outcome of the Reformation in
Germany 'were allowed to disappear'.[6] It was not in
Germany nor out of Lutheranism that the first pacifists
of the Reformation were to arise.

For them we turn to Switzerland. Here the Reformation was distinctly more thorough, giving indeed their
name to the 'Reformed' Churches which trace their

origin to the leadership of Zwingli in Zürich and later
of Calvin in Geneva. It is difficult to suppose that
Zwingli ever came in sight of anything resembling
genuine pacifism. The fine statue of him at Zürich
shows him with a Bible in one hand and with a sword
in the other, and very truthfully; and the sword is by
no means only the sword of the Spirit. Like so many
of his countrymen, who were then known as 'the
mercenaries of Europe', Zwingli had served as a
soldier, and as a soldier he died in 1531, when not
yet 50, 'at the head of the army of Zurich on the
battlefield of Cappel'.[7] It is true that for a time, at the
beginning of his reforms, Zwingli was not only 'the
leader of the friends of peace in Switzerland'[8], but was
associated with a Bible-study circle in which 'the
pacifist view-point was present'.[9] But this was in the
initial period during which he was content to study
Scripture and to preach against the Mass. When
after four years of this he found that 'nothing hap-
pened; everything remained as it was', he grew
impatient for 'practical reform'; but 'the . . . situation
in Zurich was such that he could not proceed without
the consent of the civil authorities' who had now seized
the ecclesiastical jurisdiction formerly exercised by the
Bishop of Constance. When 'it became clear that in
spite of Zwingli's' 'willingness to proceed, the' city
'council preferred to postpone action', he decided
to 'wait for official action'. In terms of his own purpose,
his desire for the council's co-operation may seem
wholly admirable; but what he did, as Professor
Bender points out, was 'to subordinate the work of
reform, and therewith the life of the church, to the
authority and power of the civil state, and in effect to

adopt the principle of the state church'.[10] As in Luther's case, there was a demonstrable change in his conception of the Church.[11] Although Zwingli 'continued to uphold in theory the sole authority of the Scripture in the life of the church, in practice he made the authority of the Council the final . . . authority';[12] and by his action, as by Luther's alliance with the 'godly prince', pacifism was again ruled out. We witness in him 'a gradual transition to the use of force in religious matters'. As we shall see, he 'turned to forceful measures to maintain his position in Zurich as well as to promote and defend the Reformation in Switzerland';[13] and it was not long before he 'was actively engaged in planning a great military alliance to fight the pope'.[14]

Meanwhile, the Bible-study group in Zürich to which I referred earlier had been gaining in members and momentum, the members including, along with a number of tradespeople, two young university students, Felix Manz and Conrad Grebel, who expounded the Bible to the others in Hebrew and Greek respectively. For some time they remained Zwingli's friends and admirers; but, when Zwingli 'put the state in a position of dominance in the life of the church', Grebel saw 'the issue and . . . put the challenge to Zwingli publicly and irrevocably. . . . The two men made opposite decisions and from here their ways separated'.[15] The actual break came over the practice of baptism. Grebel and his friends, like other close students of the Bible at this time, began to withhold their children from infant baptism, which Zwingli and the City Fathers 'had definitely decided to retain';[16] and after fruitless endeavours to persuade the dissenters by disputations, during the winter of 1524–5, the Council gave them eight days to be gone from Zürich. They did go, after first holding a service of believers' baptism, but not for long; by November 1525 Grebel and Manz were both back in Zürich and were both thrown into prison there. In the following March the Council sternly forbade the practice of rebaptism, declaring death by drowning to be the penalty for disobedience; nor did they intend this as a mere threat: less than a year later Manz actually suffered drowning, thus becoming 'the first martyr of the Anabaptists in Zurich'.[17] Grebel himself actually died of the plague a little earlier, before he was 30; but another of the group was burnt at the stake at Schwyz, and in Professor Bender's words, 'the further history of the Anabaptist movement became chiefly a record of martyrdom'.[18]

It is a terrible story; though no more terrible than other stories of persecution to the death by Christians of Christians: by the Inquisition in Spain, by Calvin in Geneva, or in this country by Roman Catholics of Protestants during Mary's reign, and by Protestants of Roman Catholics during Elizabeth's. That in a world so fierce and so sure of itself, and so sure, too, of the effectiveness of compulsion, pacifist convictions should be held by anyone is surely remarkable. There is no need to vilify Zwingli and the Zürich City Council. They, too, shared to a large degree in the vision of the Reformation. As Rufus Jones well says, 'those who had this vision, and with it had the power of restraint, and the gifts of statesmanship to see what would *work* and what would not work in the world as it actually was then, became the leaders of the Protestant Reformation, and have their renown in the pages of history. Those who had this vision', he goes on, 'and who were re- solved to *make the world fit the vision*, with no shade of levelling down and with no hairsbreadth of a com- promise, became the leaders of Anabaptism, risked everything for the cause they believed in, flung out ideals which have been guiding stars for us ever since, went to death in terrible fashions, and fell on almost total obscurity'.[19] To Conrad Grebel and his friends there trace their origin, so far as historical continuity is concerned, not only the Baptists throughout the world and indeed all Free Churches existing in separation from the State, but also our modern Christian Pacifist movement; which is why, for our purpose here, I have spent so long on the circumstances of the Reformation in general, and in Zürich in particular, in which they came into being.

'The pacifist view-point was present', as I said earlier, in the Bible-study group which first drew them to- gether. Andreas Castelberger, the Zürich bookseller who initiated their meetings, 'said much about war', a friend reported: 'how the divine teaching is so strong against it and how it is sin; and he expressed the idea that the soldier who . . . received money and pay to kill innocent persons . . . was . . . according to the content of Gospel teaching . . . a murderer . . . regard- less of the fact that this might not be so according to human laws'.[20] How far such revolutionary teaching was immediately acceptable to the group as a whole does not appear; but it is noticeable that Grebel, who 'from the beginning' was 'recognized as the leader' of the wider group that quickly formed, 'took no part in' the 'acts of' iconoclasm and 'violence' which

accompanied the Reformation's onset in Zürich as
elsewhere. The group's pacifism is strikingly expressed
in a letter sent in 1524 to Thomas Münzer, a too eager
spirit who as they knew had been cast off by Luther
as they had been by Zwingli, a letter written by Grebel
but signed also by Manz, Castelberger and others.
'The Gospel and those who accept it', they wrote, 'are
not to be protected by the sword, nor are they thus
to protect themselves. . . . Truly believing Christians
are sheep among wolves, sheep for the slaughter;
anguish and affliction, tribulation, persecution, suffering and death must be their baptism; they must be
tried with fire, and must reach the fatherland of eternal
rest, not by killing their bodily, but by mortifying their
spiritual enemies. Neither do they use worldly sword
or war, since by them killing is entirely abrogated'.[21]
Not content with this, Grebel added a postscript
lamenting the news that Münzer was advocating the
use of violence against the civil authorities in Germany
(he was in fact encouraging the Peasants' Revolt).
'If thou art willing to defend war', Grebel wrote, 'then
I admonish thee . . . that thou cease therefrom. . . .
And if thou must suffer for it, know well that it cannot
be otherwise. Christ must yet more suffer in His
members. But He will strengthen and keep them steadfast to the end'.[22]

The emphasis in all this, as you will have noted, is
different from the emphasis in the pacifism of the
mediæval sects which we considered in the last lecture.
The emphasis is upon suffering, the necessity for
suffering, in the Christian ethic. 'It is noteworthy',
Professor Bender writes, 'that Grebel bases his rejection
of the sword and war and of killing as a whole, not

upon the specific teaching of the Sermon on the Mount
but upon the thought of the suffering church'.[23] 'In all
the extant writings of Grebel, including his letters', he
adds, 'there is not one quotation from the Sermon on
the Mount, and there is no evidence that this portion
of the teaching of Christ exerted an outstanding influence on his ethical and religious thinking more
than any other portion of the New Testament'.[24] As
'a believer in the principle of biblical non-resistance',
'Grebel derived his conviction primarily from the central
thought of "the suffering church" '.[25] This thought
is something new in the development of our study.
Whether it originated in Grebel's mind we cannot tell.
It is just possible that it originated in Zwingli's mind.
Zwingli had a friend, Myconius, who was also a friend
of Grebel's; and in 1520, when Myconius was then
suffering persecution for having adopted the Reformed faith at Lucerne (where in his student days
Grebel had climbed Pilatus with him), Zwingli wrote
to Myconius: 'there will always be people who will
persecute us Christians because Christ is in us. . . . I
believe that just as the church was born in blood, so it
can be renewed only by blood, not otherwise. . . .
Never will the world accept Christ, and even the
promise of rewards by Christ is accompanied by the
promise of persecution. He sent out His own like sheep
among wolves.'[26] If Zwingli at one time shared
Grebel's thought of a Suffering Church it would
explain the acute bitterness he later betrays towards
Grebel, who had held fast to it, when Zwingli had
abandoned it. However that may be, it is Grebel who
draws out its implications for the repudiation not only
of persecution but of war. In any case, it is perhaps

needless to look for influences upon Grebel of other minds. Professor Bender concludes his biography of him with the considered judgement that 'Grebel and his Swiss Brethren derived their faith solely and directly from the New Testament without any apparent literary or personal antecedents'.[27] 'The Zurich Anabaptist group', he says, 'was autochthonous',[28] and their 'broad ideal of absolute love and non resistance rejecting war and violence in every form, both political and personal' was 'an outstandingly unique contribution'.[29]

I have called the title of this lecture, 'The Ministry of Suffering'. If we were to limit ourselves solely to Grebel and his immediate circle, I am not altogether sure that the word 'ministry' in the title would be in place. For, if I may quote what I have written elsewhere on this subject: 'An unsympathetic observer might remark that in their acceptance of suffering the Swiss Brethren were doing no more than making the best of difficult circumstances. . . . It is . . . possible to practise the gospel of love for the brethren within the Church and still to show nothing warmer than resignation towards persecutors, accepting the suffering inflicted by them as the will of God but not seeing in it an opportunity of ministry towards them. . . . Even this,' it is true, ' . . . is a notable advance on . . . resentment and (a) retaliatory spirit. . . . It is . . . nearer to the endurance and long suffering which Paul advocated and practised, to the meekness of the Servant of the Lord who "shall not strive, nor cry".'[30] But it is hardly ministry.

The intention of ministry, nevertheless, was perhaps implicit in Grebel's thought; for it is prominent in the teaching of the leader who, within ten years of Grebel's premature death, arose to continue his witness in another country, the Dutchman Menno Simons, through whom the name 'Mennonites' has come ultimately to be applied to most of the pacifist Baptist groups throughout the world. The Baptists who converted Menno are said to have 'agreed virtually in doctrine and principle'[31] with the Swiss Brethren; but Menno does not seem to have been in direct association with those who remained from Grebel's group. A notable influence upon him was the terrible disaster at Münster: to some extent, it was 'out of the confusion which ensued' that he 'gathered the Anabaptists into a peaceful evangelical community'[32], much as Czelčický had done after the disaster at Tábor eighty years earlier. During Menno's lifetime the Baptists were persecuted fiercely in the Netherlands and in Germany, where he spent much of his life; several of those whom he baptized were burnt at the stake; but, although a price was set on his head and he had constantly to be on the move, he himself succeeded in preserving his freedom and lived to the relatively great age of 65.

Menno's repudiation of war, as an essential part of what Professor Bender has called 'the Anabaptist vision', was immediate, constant and complete. 'The regenerated do not go to war nor fight', he wrote. 'They are the children of peace who have beaten their swords into ploughshares and their spears into pruning-hooks, and they know of no war. . . . Since we are to be conformed to the image of Christ, how can we fight our enemies with the sword? . . . The truly baptized disciples of Christ . . . know of no weapons other than patience, hope, non-resistance and God's Word. . . .

We do not combat with carnal, but with spiritual weapons, with patience and with the Word of the Lord, trusting in Christ, against the flesh, the world and the devil. Nor shall there ever be found other weapons with us. Therefore be not afraid of us . . . for we do not desire your destruction but your regeneration.' It is here that we are aware of a new note; and it is often sounded. 'Our weapons', he writes, ' . . . are weapons to . . . break the flinty hearts that have never been affected by the heavenly dew of the holy word.' 'All who accept our teaching in the power of it will by God's grace not have any ill will to any one upon earth, and not against their most bitter enemies. . . . True Christians know of no vengeance, however they may be wronged; . . . They do not cry for vengeance, as the world does, but with Christ they pray, "Father, forgive them, for they know not what they do".'[33] It is good to hear these last words brought into the pacifist treasury.

We must not expect too much, even of Menno and his immediate followers. A measure of toleration for Anabaptists came first in his native land, where in the States of Holland as early as 1575 they were granted exemption from military service. Even so, 'they had no civil rights, and had to endure much oppressive treatment from orthodox Calvinism.'[34] In Switzerland there was no legal place for them till as late as 1710. So long as men remain hunted heretics, even when the perpetual danger of execution has been lessened, they are not likely to have much opportunity for ministry to their persecutors, even if in theory they come to desire it. There is, nevertheless, surely much in the pacifist witness of the sixteenth-century

Anabaptists which must arouse our admiration and make us pause for thought and rather shameful self-examination. The principle of *willingness* to suffer for Christ's sake goes very deep in our Christian faith; yet we most of the time show very little awareness that it exists. Does the fact that in this country our faith, whatever its peculiarities, be it Baptist, be it pacifist, is now tolerated, by taking away our opportunity to accept suffering for Christ's sake, weaken our principles or at least deprive us of a means of witness and ministry and persuasion? I think it may do.

I confess I am a good deal puzzled why some should think that the call to suffering in the totalitarian state is something new and fundamentally different. The situation, the form, is different, yes; and very different from what we now living in this country have known; but the principle is not different from what these earlier people had to face, and seem to have been so much clearer about facing than we are inclined to be: including the involvement of others, more especially the members of their own families. From the beginning, where Christianity has been new and living, a man's foes have been those of his own household—both in the sense that the unconverted brother has betrayed the brother to death and the father the son, and in the sense that the Christian has had to seem a foe to his Christian brother by involving him in the peril encompassing himself. The severity of Jesus is a very terrifying thing. 'Let me first go bid them farewell, which are at home at my house.' 'Lord, suffer me first to go and bury my father.' But Jesus will not have it. 'If a man love father or mother more than me, he is not worthy of me.' It is worth noting that it is not wife and children of whom Jesus speaks here, but father and mother, responsibility for whom is one of the Ten Commandments which Jesus reiterates. Yet even this prime responsibility and loyalty falls before loyalty to Jesus, to His call, to what is right.

Jesus' own crucifixion, if they had remained loyal, would have involved His loved disciples also. Indeed I think that that was a part of the bitterness He shrank from drinking: that either they would betray Him or else He, in the other sense, would betray them to death. And again and again in Christian history those who have stood firm in their witness to principle have had to leave widows and children in a state of want and defencelessness: I could refer you to letters and diaries in different centuries in which the anguish of mind over just this point is expressed most poignantly. Such men are prepared to break bad laws, and to *abide the consequences*. The consequences to *themselves*, to their own personalities, if it is persecution and not martyrdom, may well be bad; though, if they accept them in the right spirit, they will not be. Persecution primarily accentuates what is there already: it hardens those who are already hard, the embittered it makes bitterer: but it further ennobles the noble spirit, and purifies the pure in heart to see God in their sufferings. 'There was never yet any prisons or sufferings that I was in,' writes George Fox the Quaker, 'but still it was for the bringing multitudes more *out* of prison.'[35] The consequences to *others* these men also accept; and that, undoubtedly, is often harder. But they none of them judge the rightness or wrongness of what they do by looking at the consequences. The consequences, which we cannot tell anyway, however tempted we are to speculate about them, have to be left to God.

All this suffering and involving others in suffering is no monopoly of Christian Pacifists; but because in this country we in this generation have no experience of persecution and suffering for Christ's sake, we tend, like our non-pacifist brethren, to shun the remembrance of its prominence in the New Testament and in almost every generation down to our own. It is the Swiss Brethren and the Mennonites who above all call us, not only in practice but in *principle*, to be *willing* to suffer for Christ's sake, yes even if it should mean (as for them it nearly always did mean) involving those whom we love most dearly.

The other question these men leave uneasily in my mind is how far they were right to believe that true Christians will *always* be persecuted by the world. 'There will *always* be people who will persecute us Christians because Christ is in us.' 'The Son of man *must* suffer.' 'In the world ye shall have tribulation'; 'blessed are ye, when men shall hate you'; 'behold, I send you forth as sheep among wolves.' Do the tenses here point to occasion only, or do they point to necessity and the nature of the case? Frankly, I am not sure; and the Swiss Brethren will not allow me to let the matter rest.

NOTES

[1] R. J. Smithson, *The Anabaptists*, p. 85.
[2] E. Troeltsch, ii. 692.
[3] *ibid.*, 694.
[4] H. A. Bender, *The Anabaptist Vision*, p. 12.
[5] E. Troeltsch, ii. 948.
[6] *ibid.*, ii. 694.
[7] H. A. Bender, *Conrad Grebel*, p. 201.

[8] *ibid.*, p. 274.
[9] *ibid.*, p. 201.
[10] *ibid.*, p. 92.
[11] *ibid.*, p. 93.
[12] *ibid.*, p. 253.
[13] *ibid.*
[14] *ibid.*, p. 201.
[15] *ibid.*, p. 99.
[16] *ibid.*, p. 136.
[17] *ibid.*, p. 160.
[18] *ibid.*, p. 153.
[19] R. M. Jones, *Studies in Mystical Religion*, p. 371.
[20] H. A. Bender, *Conrad Grebel*, p. 200.
[21] cf. *ibid.*, pp. 284 f.
[22] cf. *ibid.*, pp. 286 f.
[23] *ibid.*, p. 179.
[24] *ibid.*, p. 202.
[25] *ibid.*
[26] *ibid.*, p. 93.
[27] *ibid.*, p. 214.
[28] *ibid.*, p. 274.
[29] *ibid.*, p. 211.
[30] *Studies in Christian Social Commitment*, ed. John Ferguson, p. 83.
[31] J. Horsch, *Menno Simons*, p. 31.
[32] E. Troeltsch, ii. 705.
[33] J. Horsch, *Menno Simons*, pp. 281–6.
[34] E. Troeltsch, ii. 705.
[35] G. Fox, *Journal*, ed. N. Penney, ii. 338 (spelling modernized and italics mine.)

IV

THE DIGNITY OF MAN

IN this country the pacifist interpretation of the Christian Gospel is peculiarly associated with the Society of Friends or Quakers. 'Are you faithful in maintaining our testimony against all war as inconsistent with the spirit and teaching of Christ? Do you live in the life and power that takes away the occasion of all wars?' Once a year these questions, among other 'Queries' as they are called, are read aloud in every Friends' Meeting for Worship; and every Friend who pays attention is reminded both that the Society to which he belongs bears a testimony against war corporately, and that upon himself personally lies a responsibility to be faithful in maintaining it. The actual wording of the Query is fairly recent, but its substance is far from recent. Already in the eighteenth century Friends could speak of 'our ancient testimony' against war; and as a body the Society has been steadfast in bearing it throughout the now more than three hundred years of its history. It is perhaps worth dwelling upon, that this relatively small body of Christians has stood faithful for so long; for, while within this period pacifist convictions have slowly spread in the older Christian communions, no new Christian community with any comparable influence has arisen for which pacifism is equally central.

When Friends first drew together to form a fresh Christian group, it was in a time when men had recently been at each other's throats, in the fury of Civil War, and when the country was still held in the divisive hatred of the war's aftermath. In the second lecture we saw the Bohemian Brethren gathering about Czelčický after the Taborite Wars; in the last lecture we saw the Dutch Anabaptists gathering about Menno Simons after the disaster at Münster; now we see the English Friends gathering about George Fox after the execution of Charles I in 1649 and Cromwell's following victories at Dunbar and Worcester. We have grown used to thinking of Quakers as essentially pacific folk. Three hundred years of discipline may have made them so; but they were not so in the beginning—not, I mean, people who had always been peace-loving and were so by nature. On the contrary, as William Penn says of them in his introduction to Fox's *Journal*, 'they were changed men': 'they were changed men themselves', he says, 'before they went about to change others.'[1] I think it is not generally realized how many of them had been soldiers or sailors before they became Friends. In an appendix to her fine study entitled, *The Quakers in Peace and War*, Miss Hirst names nearly a hundred in the first generation of Friends of whom this is true. The list includes such leaders as James Nayler, Richard Hubberthorne and William Dewsbury; and there is no reason to suppose that there were not many more besides those of whom we happen to know. Fox himself says that when he was in prison at Derby in 1650, among men pressed to be soldiers, 'they would have had me to be captain of them, to go forth to Worcester fight, and the soldiers cried they would have none but me'.[1a] But Fox would never serve. His was not a spirit which readily served any man; and, as he says on more than one occasion, 'The postures of war I never learned'.[2] The phrase is characteristic in its suggestion that he had got *beyond*, or perhaps better *behind*, war. He says of a trooper who came under his influence in Derby prison that he 'saw to the end of fighting.'[3] For Fox it was not war in itself which was out of the question, so much as the attitudes of mind and spirit which dispose men to war, and without which war would not be possible. Again and again he refers to 'the occasion of all wars'; and adventurous and advanced as his thinking in the social and economic spheres often was, he is here not thinking in these terms at all; he is thinking in the religious terms natural to one who, as he already told the soldiers at Derby, had been brought into 'the virtue of that life and power that took away the occasion of all wars'.[4] It was a matter of 'life and power'.

There is much in George Fox and early Quakerism which reminds us of the mediæval sects and their dependence upon 'the law of Christ' in the New Testament. 'Though the Bible were lost, it might be found in the mouth of George Fox',[4a] a contemporary said of him; and in justification of his repudiation of war, as of much else besides, Fox often refers to the teaching of Jesus, and especially to the Sermon on the Mount. (At the Mount School, the Quaker girls' school in York, there is still a tradition that the Sermon on the Mount may be learned by heart, and a prize is offered for those who can recite it.) Fox's attitude to Scripture is nevertheless radically different from (say) John Wycliffe's. Fox no longer sees Christian discipleship primarily in terms of obedience to law. It is something much freer and more adventurous. He seized

hold of the Reformation assurance that God's Holy
Spirit was given livingly to every man to answer to
His Word in the Bible; and in the light of that Spirit,
the living Spirit of the Risen Christ, he gave himself
up to walk till travelling days were done. There is
about Fox a wonderful resilience. 'I never saw him
out of his place', Penn writes, 'or not a match for every
service or occasion.'[5] And he *could* be thus because
he was utterly sure of certain principles which were
fundamental and unchanging. One was that this
'spirit and power' by which he lived had not been
given to him alone, it was for everyman. He had the
genius, which means the combination of humility with
faith, to universalize his experience. As Penn tersely
puts it, 'the principle is one in all'.[5a] Another was that
the Spirit of Christ and 'the occasion of all wars' were
clean contrary the one to the other. To quote a fine
sentence which Fox wrote in 1657: 'All dwelling in the
light that comes from Jesus, leads out of wars': 'leads
out of strife', he continues, 'leads out of the occasion
of wars, and leads out of the earth, up to God, out
of earthly mindedness into heavenly mindedness, and
brings your minds to be in heaven'.[6] The conflation
of biblical references here is of a piece with the largeness and *wholeness* of Fox's mind, in which the repudiation of war falls naturally into place as a part, a neces-
sary part, but no more than a part, of a larger whole.

Without this largeness of outlook, it is unlikely that
Fox would have attracted to himself, as he did, a fellowship of such varying gifts and temperaments, all
united in unshakeable devotion to the same fundamental principles. William Charles Braithwaite, the
historian of early Quakerism, draws attention to the

remarkable unanimity of Friends over matters which then, as now, divide most Christians;[7] and one of these was the Christian attitude to war. Of course there were backslidings, as in the case of the Westmorland Friend, Thomas Ayrey, that 'poor fainting man', who, it is written, 'could suffer nothing for Truth' and 'when like to suffer for Truth's testimony against fighting and bearing outward arms, . . . consented to take arms';[8] and, of course, there were hesitations, as when Francis Gawler wrote to Fox of his non-Quaker brother, 'His colonel is a loving man to Friends, and is very desirous to have Friends in his regiment . . . but Friends are not free to meddle with it, only Matthew Gibbon hath partly engaged to be a captain.' But on the back of this letter, which still exists, Fox scrawled, 'which G. F. forbade and said it was contrary to our principles; for our weapons are spiritual and not carnal';[9] and within ten years of Friends' coming into being, 'The Spirit of Christ', they said, in a printed *Declaration* signed by Fox and Hubberthorne and ten other Friends, 'The Spirit of Christ, by which we are guided . . . which leads us into all truth, will never move us to fight and war against any man with outward weapons, neither for the kingdom of Christ nor for the kingdoms of this world.'[10] Friends also excelled in the quality of their fellowship one with another, and in the lengths they would go in expressing it, 'body for body'.

Fox himself remained all his life—to use words of his own about another early leader, Robert Widder— 'a thundering man'.[11] It is perhaps not so surprising that when he came to York in 1652 they flung him down the steps of the South Transept entrance. 'He is as stiff as a tree', said some soldiers of him at Scarborough, 'and as pure as a bell; for we could never stir him.'[12] What in my introduction to the 1952 edition of his *Journal* I have called his 'forbearance' is the more striking; and indeed there are occasions when he goes far past forbearance, and the acceptance of suffering, in an outward-going 'love to them all that had persecuted me'.[13] Yet for all his winning qualities, there is, one must admit, a certain hardness about Fox—as perhaps there will be about almost any leader and organizer of men. If one cannot exactly say of his writings what Miss Hirst says of the letters of another leader, Edward Burrough, that they 'show a fondness for military metaphor',[14] there is plenty in them to the tone and tune of trampling down evil. I do not mean you to think that I find this out of place. I find it immensely inspiriting. But it was left to other leaders to reflect more *obviously* in *character* the gentleness and peaceable spirit to which Fox constantly appealed as that which excluded the possibility of war. James Nayler, a Yorkshireman from Wakefield, who in the earliest days had a position among Friends to be compared with Fox's, is the outstanding name here, as is that of John Woolman in the eighteenth century. Nayler could appeal to men to put on Christ 'so plentifully that you may have (wherewith) to cast over a brother's nakedness a garment of the same love, who came from above to lay down his life for his enemies, and of the same power who can forgive sins and offences above seven times a day, beholding each other with that good eye which waits for the soul and not for the sin, which covers and overcomes the evil with the good'.[15] Here, springing from a soul of great gentleness, is the life and power which takes away the occasion of all wars. Beside it I put the following description of Friends written in 1661 from prison at Aylesbury by a lesser-known early leader, John Whitehead, who, again, had at one time been a soldier: 'in the furnace of affliction, where judgement and mercy meets, they are melted into tenderness, and bowels of pity are opened in them towards all creatures, but especially mankind . . . they have compassion on them that are out of the way . . . they cannot seek the destruction of sinners though they be obstinate, but rather that they may have time and space to repent, and be turned to the Lord; and being leavened throughout with love and mercy, it is against their very nature to revenge themselves, or use carnal weapons to kill, hurt or destroy mankind . . . having received forgiveness of their trespasses, they are ready to forgive them that trespass against them; and do with their hearts love their enemies, and are ready to spend and be spent for the good of their souls'.[16]

In these last passages we have sounding quietly but to the full those combined notes of compassion and suffering love and of overcoming the world which mark Christian Pacifism at its noblest. In its consciousness of being a separated society over against the world—Aldous Huxley has used of the Society the striking phrase 'fanatically marginal'[17]—in its constant reference back to the New Testament, the Sermon on the Mount and the Spirit of Christ, in its meek acceptance of suffering and its irrepressible desire to serve and to save men, Quakerism takes its place in the historic succession we have been studying, which in our own time we long to carry farther. But that which is peculiarly the Quaker contribution is perhaps none of these things. It is something nearer to what I have called, in the title of this lecture, 'The Dignity of Man'. Friends, like all the seventeenth-century Puritans, of whom, when they arose, they were the most radical representatives, were children of the Reformation; but they were also influenced deeply, and more deeply than they knew, by the Renaissance. The Renaissance was a movement of learning, the leaders of which had gone back to the fountain-head of much that is finest in the culture of the West by studying classical antiquity in the writings of the Greeks and Romans, much as the Reformers had done in their recovery of the Bible in its original tongues. Now very few of the early Quakers were learned, or even scholarly, men. True; but the study of the ancient world had brought about, as it is still wont to do, a new respect for personality and a new faith in the capacities of man, which in the seventeenth century was increasingly in the air men breathed, whether or not they had been to one of the many grammar schools founded as one result of the new movement; and Friends' repudiation of war as an affront to the human soul was at least, in part, a reflection of this humanism.

In certain circles to-day humanism is under a cloud, and not entirely without reason. When humanism means a pretence to human self-sufficiency and all-sufficiency over against God, it is an ugly thing and a pathetic. But a Christian humanism which asks reverently, 'What is man, that *thou* art mindful of him? *Thou* madest him . . .', and which believes that in Jesus 'the Son of Man' the Divine dwelt among men, will, by respecting the highest in man, call forth the

best in man and will express itself in dispositions of
humanity and humanitarianism. In the Scottish universities the classics are still known as 'the humani-
ties'; and it is not surprising if those who through Plato
find a natural and universal dignity within the human
soul, who through Aristotle admire the heights to
which human reason can attain, who in the poetry of
Vergil hear 'the still sad music of humanity', follow
lines of thought which bring them to abhor the unworthy and unreasonable self-slaughter which war is.
Thus in the sixteenth century Erasmus, who perhaps
represents the Christian humanist at his best, and whose
influence in this country was very great, was pro-
nounced in his abhorrence of it. The Bible-study group
at Zürich admired Erasmus greatly; and it is not
unlikely that they were influenced by Erasmus' tract,
The Complaint of Peace, which has often been reprinted
as peace propaganda, and by another tract against
war by his friend Myconius, which, though unpublished,
it is known that Conrad Grebel read.[18] 'How can you
say "Our Father",' Erasmus writes, 'while you are
thrusting the sharp steel into the body of your
brother?'[19] At the same time Professor Bender acutely
distinguishes Erasmus' pacifism from that of the Swiss
Brethren. 'Even though there is a religious tone and
coloring in Erasmus' thought on the question of war
and peace', he says, 'nevertheless the Erasmian pacifism
was primarily humanitarian in character and not
theological and biblical. . . . Erasmus, although he
at times used very sharp words against war, was ready
not only to permit a defensive war, but even any just
war.'[20]

In the seventeenth century Erasmian humanism had penetrated widely and can be seen as an influence in many spheres. Jan Comenius, the last leader of the Bohemian Brethren before they went underground during a century of terrible persecution, owed much to him; and Comenius was an educationalist of international repute, whose temper and ideals, while markedly and thoroughly pacific, are more in line with those of Erasmus than of Czelčický. The Italian Fausto Sozzini, whose followers, the Socinians, were the spiritual ancestors of those now called Unitarians, is another whom the claims of reason as much as the spirit of Christ led to repudiate war. *The Racovian Catechism*, published in 1605 at Racow by the Polish Socinians, is perhaps the first official document of the kind in Christian history to declare war unlawful. In the Netherlands, once more, the pacifism of a fresh offshoot of the Anabaptist movement, the followers of Gisbert van der Kodde, known as the Collegianten, is considerably different in tone from that of the Swiss Brethren a hundred years earlier. They too had come under Socinian influence; and their doctrine of *weerloosheid* or 'defencelessness' is as much a principle of reason and humanity as of faith and divine injunction.[21] Something of the same approach is apparent later on, in the eighteenth century, in the teaching of the German philosopher, Immanuel Kant. 'So act', wrote Kant, 'that you treat humanity, whether in your own person or in the person of every one else, always as an end, never merely as a means.' One is not surprised to read that Kant, who wrote a work *Concerning Perpetual Peace*, had a 'peculiar hatred of war', calling it 'the scourge of mankind', 'making more bad men than it takes away', and 'the destroyer of every good'.[22] The lines from the eighteenth-century English poet, William Blake, are in the same tradition:

> And all must love the human form
> In heathen, Turk or Jew.

While Christians for so many centuries had found it hard to love, instead of persecuting, one another, they could hardly be expected to love the heathen, Turk or Jew. But this was at last breaking through. With very little exception there was no Protestant missionary enterprise until about the time of Kant and Blake. But now, at the very end of the eighteenth century, a missionary society was provided by the Baptists, who thus were pioneers here as earlier in Christian Pacifism.

But to return to the seventeenth century and to Friends. I think it is evident that, largely without knowing it, the Quakers—even the first Quakers—had absorbed something of this humanism. Much of their later humanitarian activities—the part they played in the struggle to abolish the slave trade and slavery itself, for instance, or their pioneer work in the care of the insane in York at The Retreat—has some of its roots here. Only, where Erasmus and those in his line are generally called Christian humanists, the Quakers may rather be called humane Christians. The fact that the appellation now sounds odd is an index of the measure of the harvest which they have reaped during these last three hundred years. Christians have by no means always been humane; indeed, from that important date near the beginning of our studies, A.D. 313, when Christianity became the religion of the State, the persecution of Christians by Christians, let alone of unbelievers by Christians, makes a great part of the tragic story of 'man's inhumanity to man'. You can see that men could hardly be brought to repudiate war till they first so learned to respect man as man that they repudiated persecution. To-day, in Protestant countries, toleration, and the respect and tolerance which make toleration possible, have won the day; and to that conquest also the Quakers have contributed greatly. The growth of indifference, the weakening of faith, have contributed too, admittedly; but, even where men still believe passionately and care greatly, they have come to see that persecution is both unreasonable and wrong and, by exercising forbearance, to refrain from it. It is easy enough to believe in a thing passionately and to try to force it on others. It is also easy enough to be indifferent. It is difficult to believe in a thing passionately and to want others to believe in it too, but still to respect their personality and spiritual autonomy and seek only to persuade them, and to win their willing mind. Taking the Christian era as a whole, this is such a recent and revolutionary thing that it may enhearten us to hope that in time men will look upon war as they now look upon persecution.

The Renaissance strain in Quakerism is most evident in its 'universal' note. Only, where the humanists built their arguments on the universality of reason in men, Friends built theirs on the universality in men of the Spirit of God, or the Spirit or Light of Christ as they called it. This conviction that there is a divine spark kindled in all men—'that of God in everyman'—is really the first-principle in Quakerism, from which everything else flows. It produced in them a strange

new Christian egalitarianism, both among themselves
and towards others. Among themselves, if it was not
always true that, as William Dewsbury claimed, 'the
mistress and maid are hail-fellow well met',[23] at least
in Meeting for Worship they were at one, and vocal
ministry might be the gift and duty of the maid rather
than of her mistress or master; as also in the Burial
Ground, where no distinctions of wealth or position
were allowed, the burial stones, if there were any, being
strictly identical in shape and size. Towards outsiders,
the titles and manners by which difference of rank
were conventionally indicated were dispensed with:
they were an affront on the Divine image, which was
present in all men equally, not in one more than
another. And what in this negative form was easily
misunderstood by others as no more than discourtesy
and impertinence took a more obviously positive
expression in Friends' readiness to take their message
to all men, of whatever rank or nation or race. In
Edward Grubb's words, 'the fervent belief that the
Light was given in measure to all men raised all human
personality to a new dignity. Not Christians only, but
Jews, Turks, Indians, savages, had something of God
in them and something that could appreciate and would
respond to truth and justice and goodwill.'[24]

I suppose that the best known example of carrying
such a belief into practice is to be found in William
Penn's treaty with the Indians in 1682. 'The Great
Spirit who made me and you', Penn told the Indians,
'... knows that I and my friends have a hearty desire
to live in peace and friendship with you, and to serve
you to the utmost of our power. It is not our custom
to use hostile weapons against our fellow creatures, for

which reason we have come unarmed. . . . I will consider you as the same flesh and blood with the Christians, and the same as if one man's body were to be divided into two parts.'[25] This, you will agree, is great humanism. It is also great Christianity; but it would hardly be possible, historically speaking, without the respect for man as man which at the Renaissance was regained from the ancient world. It was a pagan poet, you remember, on whom Paul drew long before at Athens to support his thesis that God had 'made of one blood all nations of men . . . that they should seek the Lord, if haply they might feel after him, and find him'.

I do not want to exaggerate the importance of this aspect. Had I been giving a single lecture on the Quaker testimony against war, the proportions would have been different, and I might hardly have mentioned it; but within our studies as a whole it is right, I think, to bring out this new sense of the dignity of man as a jewel first finding its shining place in the pacifist treasury through Quakerism. Friends have never forgotten the limiting phrase in St. Paul's injunction, to 'do good unto all men, especially unto them who are of the household of faith': in the care of their own members they have set standards far above the other Churches. But, in words of Fox as noble as they are simple, 'We love all men and women, simply as they are men and women, and as they are God's workmanship, and so as brethren'.[26] 'Honouring all men', he says elsewhere, 'is reaching that of God in every man';[27] and again, 'patience must get the victory, and answers to that of God in everyone, and will bring everyone from the contrary'.[28]

Alfred Neave Brayshaw, the biographer of Fox and historian of Quakerism, insists on the centrality in Fox's thought of this conception of 'that of God in everyman'; and as it was from Neave Brayshaw that I first gained some understanding both of Quakerism and of pacifism, it is natural that I should do so too. 'The Quaker testimony concerning war', Neave Brayshaw writes, ' . . . is based ultimately on the conception of "that of God in every man" to which the Christian in the presence of evil is called on to make appeal, following out a line of thought and conduct which, involving suffering as it may do, is, in the long run, the most likely to reach to the inward witness and so change the evil mind into the right mind. This result is not achieved by war'.[29] You will note here the positive evangelical purpose of the Quaker peace testimony as thus set forth. 'It was, in fact, an essentially missionary gospel which' Fox 'preached, the gospel of Christ's power to meet evil and to overcome it';[30] and his pacifism, as we saw earlier, was only a part, though an inalienable part, of that larger gospel. 'Look not at your sufferings', he wrote once, 'but at the power of God, and that will bring some good out in all your sufferings; and your imprisonments will reach to the prisoned, that the persecutor prisons in himself'.[31]

'Answering that of God' thus means *both* responding to God's seeking us and speaking to us through others *and* speaking to that of God in others, even when it is imprisoned, concealed, perhaps from their own eyes, still answering that of God which speaks in and through them, though their outer words may be in another tone and temper; and by answering it, drawing it out; in fact by liberating it, for all practical purposes creating it. Faith often creates in someone else, and so in a situation, what would not otherwise have been there.

Modern pacifism often suffers from being what looks like a 'thing', a kink, a bee in the bonnet, unrelated to the rest of our living and thinking, even to our Christian living and thinking. Perhaps the greatest challenge Quakerism makes to us is to hold fast so firmly to the great Christian centralities that pacifism issues from them naturally, no longer as something odd and un-attached, but as a matter of course; and therewith so to love all men, both as God's workmanship and as brothers for whom Christ died, that intentionally to harm them, whether by war or by any other means, is simply unthinkable. We want to help them, to win them, not to hurt them. But that is our final theme, namely, 'The Means of Redemption'.

NOTES

[1] Intro. to G. Fox, *Journal* (1901 edn.), i. xxxvii.

[1a] G. Fox, *Journal*, ed. N. Penney, i. 11 (spelling modernized).

[2] Cf. *ibid.*, i. 358–64.

[3] *ibid.*, i. 13.

[4] *ibid.*, i. 11 f.

[4a] G. Croese, *History of the Quakers*, p. 14; cit. A. N. Brayshaw, *The Personality of George Fox*, p. 16.

[5] Intro. to G. Fox, *Journal* (1901 edn.), i. l.

[5a] *ibid.*, i. xlix.

[6] Cit. M. Hirst, *The Quakers in Peace and War*, p. 114.

[7] Cf. W. C. Braithwaite, *The Beginnings of Quakerism*, p. 137.

[8] *First Publishers of Truth*, ed. N. Penney, p. 266 (spelling modernized).

[9] Cit. M. Hirst, p, 56.

[10] Cit. *ibid.*, p. 115.

[11] G. Fox, *Journal*, ed. N. Penney, i. 292.

[12] *ibid.*, ii. 104.

[13] *ibid.*, i. 58.

[14] M. Hirst, p. 120.

[15] J. Nayler, *A Message from the Spirit of Truth*, p. 8.

[16] J. Whitehead, *A Small Treatise*, pp. 14 ff.

[17] A. Huxley, *Grey Eminence*, p. 254.
[18] Cf. H. A. Bender, *Conrad Grebel*, pp. 200 f.
[19] *Erasmus on War*, ed. D. Gibb, p. 15.
[20] H. A. Bender, p. 201.
[21] Cf. C. B. Hylkema, *Reformateurs*, ii. 71 f.
[22] I. Kant, *Perpetual Peace*, tr. M. Campbell Smith, pref. by tr., p. 58.
[23] Cit. W. C. Braithwaite, *The Second Period of Quakerism*, p. 451.
[24] E. Grubb, *What is Quakerism?*, p. 125.
[25] Cit. *Friends: Some Quaker Peace Documents 1654–1920*, ed. G. W. Knowles, pp. 36 f.
[26] Cit. A. N. Brayshaw, *The Personality of George Fox*, p. 63.
[27] Cit. *ibid.*, p. 63, n. 1.
[28] Cit. *ibid.*, p. 31.
[29] *A. Neave Brayshaw: Memoir*, ed. R. Davis and R. C. Wilson, p. 131.
[30] G. Fox, *Journal*, ed. J. L. Nickalls, p. xxix.
[31] G. Fox, *Epistles*, p. 80.

V

THE MEANS OF REDEMPTION

I HOPE you will accept it as sincere in me and not mock-modesty, when I say that I find this last lecture the most difficult part of my task. Most people would suppose it to be the easiest. But what professional competence I possess lies in the study and interpretation of history, of the past: in the earlier lectures I could speak of subjects about which I do know something. Now, as I try to interpret the present generation, even the present century, I have no more special competence than any one else, and can only offer suggestions and intimations. I hope that what is true in them may be seen to be true and that mistaken, distorted or misleading ideas may be allowed to fall away.

In earlier lectures I was able in the main to follow a chronological order: except that when speaking of Quakerism I thought it best to pick up first the lines continuing from what we had seen in earlier groups, and then to describe the new understanding of the dignity of man which had come in with the Renaissance, before finally showing the effect of this on the peculiarly Quaker form of pacifism. Here my plan is different, though still simple. First, I shall remark something new in the general situation. Secondly, I shall suggest a number of contributory reasons for this. I shall then point out the centrality of the thought of redemption in much contemporary Christian Pacifist writing. In conclusion I shall offer some hesitant, but

I hope helpful, considerations concerning some of the implications for us of this central thought of redemption.

First, then, what is new in the general situation where Christian Pacifists are concerned? Surely, outstandingly, that our convictions are now held by an appreciable number of members, which includes many leaders, and are respected by a great many more, in all the Churches. We are inclined very naturally, indeed very properly, to lament what a small company we are. So we are; but in comparison with past ages how much less so than of old! This, at least, you will carry away from our study: the remembrance that in the past Christian Pacifists have been tiny and relatively insignificant groups, needing all their energies to survive at all and practically never in a position to bring pressure to bear, beyond the silent pressure of an often suffering witness; and the encouragement and the challenge, that this is no longer so. In the rank and file of the Churches Christian Pacifism has still hardly made itself felt; but at the top, among those who are widely reverenced for their saintliness, and those who exercise great influence by their speaking and writing, it has won known and notable converts in all denominations: especially, and this is the striking thing, among theologians and interpreters of the Bible.

It is the same with the World Council of Churches. In its meetings the question of the Christian attitude to war is fully accepted as an issue prominent among those which must trouble the Christian conscience and be wrestled with. At Amsterdam the World Council went to far as to declare that 'war is contrary to the will of God'. How it is that the Council can leave it there, and be (seemingly) content to rest in permission for Christians to take part in a known sin, some writers even defending this very formula, is a painful mystery to us; but this should not blind us to the fact that the Protestant Churches in general, in the persons of many of their leaders and also in their official pronouncements, have come much closer to sharing our convictions than anyone would have dared to hope fifty years ago, when in this country few pacifists existed at all outside the Society of Friends. Indeed, both in the meetings of the World Council and also in the meetings alike of the British Council of Churches and of the National Council in America, it looks as if the pacifist and near-pacifist members are gaining ground.

Now, how has all this new development come about? I want to suggest eight reasons: a number so large that I must not say much about any of them. In the first place, there has been a revival of close study of the Bible among Protestants. This began in the last century with a new historical, critical and linguistic approach, which in some ways has effected a revolution in our religion as great as that which took place at the Reformation. We are, in the main, no longer Fundamentalists. But also, within the present generation, a number of scholars have shown that it is not enough to study the Bible in a detached, intellectual, critical way. If we are Christians, we have to recover the leading themes of biblical religion, of the whole revelation of God in the Bible, and to think and live, so far as we may, in spiritual accord with and loyalty to these; and to name but one, the importance of the theme of the Suffering Servant has become increasingly evident.[1] Secondly, and alongside of this, there has been, starting with the lives of Jesus by Strauss, Renan and Seeley in the middle of the last century, an unparalleled concentration upon the first three gospels and upon the character, teaching and purpose of Jesus Himself. At the same time we have come nearer to understanding the mind and heart of St. Paul, as distinct from intellectually arranging his doctrines. Both Jesus and Paul are now studied as living personalities. This has certainly favoured our cause.

Thirdly, so far as this country is concerned, the Universities of Oxford and Cambridge, which had been closed to all but members of the Church of England, were made open to Nonconformists in 1871; and in London and in the modern universities denominational barriers have never existed. Consequently, Nonconformists, including Quakers, have for the first time been enabled to share in the best methods open to anyone of equipping their minds; and the influence of their convictions, including their pacifist convictions, has been brought to bear upon members of all denominations, in the studies begun and the friendships formed at the universities. Fourthly, within a generation of the opening to them of Oxford and Cambridge, and to some degree as a result of the impact of this on their younger members, the Society of Friends underwent a remarkable revival in the ten years from 1895 to 1905. Returning to the inspiring sources of their own history and recovering a deeply mystical sense of the empowering presence of God, Friends went out, for the first time for generations, among other Christians, seeking to spread a strong, fresh message of inward religion and Christian love, with pacifism as its natural outcome.

Fifthly, a little later but with its origins still in the years before the first World War, there was a drawing together of all the Churches, and sixthly, alongside of it, a recovery of the necessity and urgency of converting men to faith in Christ. These are now strongly represented in the world by the ecumenical movement and by the missionary movement as we know it to-day. They have lately drawn together in the close collaboration of the World Council of Churches with the International Missionary Council; and wherever work is undertaken by Christians on the international level, the wrongness of war is likely to become plain. Those who meet as brothers in Christ from many countries for common consultation cannot easily return home to prepare in measures of war against one another.

Seventhly, the occurrence of two World Wars, and the feared implications of a feared third, has brought many to give serious thought to the Christian attitude to war. This is no longer a question which circumstances permit a thinking Christian to evade; and while the evil of conscription has accentuated its sharpness in the experience of many conscripts, the recognition of conscientious objection to war has in turn roused thought in Christians of all age-groups. It has been not unusual for men offering themselves as candidates for the ministry to have been brought to a sense of their vocation while they were in the armed forces, or more recently while doing their so-called national service; and they often enter the ministry, indeed sometimes their training for it, as convinced pacifists. Eighthly, and with due modesty lastly, soon after the beginning of the First War, the Fellowship of Reconciliation was founded, and from the start it has included not only a strong proportion of Quakers but members of all the Churches. More recently, there has also been the International F.o.R., and only quite lately a drawing together in terms of their shared pacifism by the Friends, the Mennonites and the Brethren. With the I.F.o.R., these now hold international conferences; and we may certainly take heart that the excellent pamphlet put out by them entitled *Peace is The Will of God* has been thought of sufficient weight to be replied to by leading non-pacifists in the World Council. The debate, at least, is on: and we must not let it drop.

These, I believe, are some of the reasons for the new and more hopeful situation. It is indeed a remarkable change; and when I compare what the pacifist leaders in the various churches write with what the older pacifists wrote, I notice a change there too. Pacifism is no longer related to single, if important, emphases in the Bible and in theology, but to themes which are central and persistent; and above all to the theme of redemption. That present-day exponents of pacifism do this is surely excellent. It means that they are living at the heart of things and that their life and convictions, including their pacifism, are all of a piece. They are also much more likely to convince others if they relate their pacifism to what is central for all thinking and committed Christians and is thus accepted by them.

'The way of war is destructive, of Christ redemptive', writes Leyton Richards in *The Christian's Alternative to War*:

War seeks to overcome evil by the infliction of injury on the evil-doer or his agents, Jesus on the

Cross by the endurance of the utmost injury that the evil-doer cares to inflict; war treats men as things, Jesus always treated them as living souls capable of responding to the love of God; war operates by killing the enemy, Jesus sought to kill the enmity; war crushes men in order to achieve victory, Jesus lost the battle in order to win men.[2]

'Of all the religions', writes the Quaker Edward Grubb, 'it is Christianity which is in the completest sense *redemptive*: which most clearly sees God Himself as taking the initiative in recalling man into a right relation with Himself and with his fellows. . . . Here is a power, the power of unlimited love, to win the soul of man. . . . The redeeming love of God brings man, without any infringement of his free personality, into a new and higher union with Himself.'[3]

Another Friend, Carl Heath, wrote in 1947 a tract entitled, *The Redemption of Europe*. In this he says: 'Old Christendom's dire needs at present are very numerous, but above all she needs redemption. And redemption is not at all the same thing as reconstruction. . . . The syllable *empt* implies a cost. Ex-empt is to forgo the cost; redemption is to pay the cost over again. There is a suffering and costingness in all that redeems.'[4]

Dr. Norman Goodall, in a pamphlet published in 1952 entitled *Pacifism and some Christian Centralities—* what an excellent title!—says:

I feel again and again that for a Christian understanding of our problems and their remedy we keep beginning at the wrong end. We begin with man, with the intractable human situation in which we

find ourselves at this present moment in history; and
we try to work our way from that to a Christian
deduction as to what is permissible or efficacious
or right. I acknowledge the challenge which this
approach constitutes for us all. It takes history
seriously and politics responsibly, and tries to keep
the feet, even of preachers, on firm ground. But
there is firmer ground than *terra firma*: there is the
City which hath the foundations whose builder and
maker is God. And there is no realistic way (a way
conforming to ultimate Reality) out of the disorder
of man until we start with the transcendent God and
that dazzling mystery of Light from whence is given
the way, the truth and the life. All Christian ethical
insight begins here. The authentic spiritual authority
of Christian pacifism proceeds from this transcendent
God whom to proclaim and glorify in worship is our
primary duty as witnesses to the way of the Cross
and recipients of that redeeming grace which gave
evil its *coup de grace* by accepting crucifixion. [5]

These writers thus all point us to redemption; and
the same thing may be found in the books of other
pacifists, such as Professor Macgregor, Canon Raven
and Professor Ferguson. All anchor our pacifism to
God's redeeming love in Christ as shown supremely in
the Cross. All see the pacifist way as an expression of
the means of redemption.

Pacifism, as Dr. Goodall insists, is not just an appeal
to all men of good sense and common sense to follow
the way of reason and good will; nor just 'a peaceful
way of achieving what violence fails to accomplish'.
Any treatment of it 'so that it becomes predominantly

associated with a pacifying device, or a kindly spirit, or even an act of ethical obedience, fails to touch the grounds of deepest conviction or the richest springs of power'.[6] Christian Pacifism is a form of witness to the outgoing, seeking, serving, giving, forgiving, winning, rescuing, saving, redeeming love of God; and an opening of ourselves to this, that we may be used of God as His channels, instruments, means. Nor is this outgoing, redeeming love of God to be found in other religions:[7] it is His seeking and saving which is a distinguishing mark of Jesus Christ. Moreover, because as Christians we believe in the resurrection of Jesus, this is not simply an intellectual statement of a historic fact. We believe that through the Holy Spirit God still seeks and saves: still imbues the lives of the disciples of Jesus with His redeeming power, enabling us both ourselves to live, and also to help in the redemption of others, in a way not possible for those who, through ignorance, carelessness or wilfulness, close their hearts' doors to His redeeming love.

It is worth noting that this understanding of pacifism as the means of redemption gathers together and carries on all the varieties of understanding which have come to our notice in the course of our historical study. We cannot hope to redeem men, to be used by God in redeeming them, unless with the early Christians we first know to what, distinctively, and for whom, unreservedly, we would do so; unless with the mediæval sects we keep close to the Bible, the New Testament, the Sermon on the Mount, where we find our promise and pattern of redemption, and our orders for our own part in it; unless with Grebel and Menno we are willing to spend and be spent, though the more we love the less we be loved, grateful for even a small share in the fellowship of Christ's sufferings; unless with the early Quakers we think of men, simply as men, as both worth redeeming and as never past hope of redeeming. In every case, I believe, we may learn from the principles which moved and controlled these earlier pacifists. We may see all their varying sanctions taken up into our own prevailing view of that which we are vowed to as inseparable from the means of redemption.

If we think of our pacifism in this way, it helps us to keep our priorities right. We are reminded that, if we are Christian Pacifists, we are pacifists because we are Christians. It is surely small use to talk of reconciliation if, in fact, we are bitter or scornful towards other disciples of Jesus who in our judgement are mistaken at this point. We are also given the answer to the question whether reconciliation to God or reconciliation between men comes first. In the title of this Fellowship, born as it was in an agonizing endeavour to preserve fellowship at a time when all the links were being snapped, I imagine that this human fellowship was prominent in intention; but I am fairly confident that its founders, a number of whom were devoted students of the New Testament, would have said—perhaps did say—that true and lasting fellowship and reconciliation between men becomes possible only through reconciliation and fellowship with God. 'Be ye reconciled to God' is the Fellowship's fundamental message. It is only those who, because they are redeemed, are no longer at enmity with God, who also have *available* to them the new caring for others, the new joy and peace in the Holy Ghost, and the new faith and patience and sensitiveness, from which human reconciliation can spring.

I want, in conclusion, to say something about this faith and patience and sensitiveness, which all true Christians need but which we Christian Pacifists, perhaps through our very keenness, often find most difficult. We must not pretend that we know, or understand, everything, or can see the whole situation, and the whole way before us, clearly. Even intellectually, to do this is the mark of the little mind: the man who is perfectly clear about all the answers, A. D. Lindsay used to tell us at Balliol, is usually the man who has not troubled to study the question. But religiously, it is worse, it is the mark of the faithless mind. We are called to use our reason as fully and honestly as we can, certainly:

> Jesus, confirm my heart's desire
> To work and speak and *think* for Thee;

but while we are on earth, we have but faith, not sight: we have the burden of accepting much uncertainty and of venturing on what we know and proving it as we go along. This is so in all human relationships: especially in those of love we have to be content to trust; and in relationship to God faith keeps us humble, conscious of our createdness and littleness. 'Seeing that things are so', we have to say with John Bunyan, 'I will venture my eternal soul upon His word, sink or swim, come Heaven, come Hell. Lord Jesus, if thou wilt catch me, do; if not, I will venture for Thy name.' If our pacifism is to be the means of redeeming others, bringing them home to God, it will have in it much of this spirit of venture: blessed assurance, but not logical certainty. It is, I am afraid, worse than useless to tell others that our position is transparently clear; or to flatter ourselves that others do not see it only because of their sin, when the sin which closes their eyes may be our own cocksureness and insensitiveness to their need.

I never knew a man more sure of his pacifism than Neave Brayshaw—he told me he would go to the stake for the free and open meeting for worship, and I have no doubt he would have done so also for Friends' peace testimony—yet it was he who said, in a passage I have already quoted, that the peace testimony is only 'in the long run, *the most likely* to . . . change the evil mind into the right mind'. For, as he also says, 'if you are on the side of Christ in His work for the world's healing, you will know far more defeats than victories if you are only going to count the number of times. But', he adds, 'once in a while you will have your share in a victory which makes up for many defeats'.[8] 'Once in a while' is all he claims. So again, if we intend our pacifism as the means of redeeming men, it is no use to pretend that it will be a short job. Redemption, God knows, is a long job. 'To seek and to save one single lost character', says W. R. Maltby, 'is to set out upon the longest and hardest journey known to human experience, with no guarantee that the search will be rewarded or that our strength will hold out to the end'.[9] No guarantee; only faith; and patience: 'having loved his own which were in the world, he loved them unto the end': end*less* patience. If so much patience is needed for the redeeming of a single soul, what is required for the redemption of the world? And it is in the redemption of the world that as Christian Pacifists we dare to interest ourselves.

Faith; and patience; and sensitiveness. Not softness; sensitiveness. Once more, if our fundamental purpose is not just to make men friends with ourselves or with one another but to bring them home to God, it is conceivable that it may be right at times to speak sharply to them, to wake, break, shake, shame them. Their feelings may need to be hurt, if their hearts are to be tendered: it is always with the hard-hearted that God has most difficulty. It is not helpful to evade the fact that Jesus did address the Pharisees in scathing, searing language; in no sense can it be called language intended to reconcile; but it could still be an expression of the motive of redemption. If I am to be honest, I confess I wish I did not know Jesus could speak in such terms; but I am prepared to believe that He did; and I am helped a little by having once taken a fellow-student who was talking of committing suicide to a well-trusted physician of souls. The minister 'attacked' the student in a way which both scared and shocked me, but was evidently an expression of sensitiveness to the man's need; for it was effective in bringing him to himself and in rescuing him from the pit—in this case the pit of self-pity—into which he was letting himself down. The difficulty with most of us is that we take so long to learn not to speak sharply to people from the wrong motives that we have little time left to learn to be able to do so on rare occasions from the right motives; and that we do not put ourselves freely and fully enough at the disposal of God's redeeming power, to direct what we say and how we say it, in sensitiveness to the needs of those with whom we have to do.

The general title of this conference has been 'The Power of Minorities'. The title is, perhaps deliberately, somewhat ambiguous. Any minority can have power, often an evil power, by being determined and closely organized; that, clearly, is not our concern. In terms of our concern I interpret the title in two ways. At one end there is the power of God, the redeeming power of God. Without this all our plans and activities are little worth and will dissolve in a thin humanism and an idealism no more than pathetic; but with it there is no end to the possibilities before us. 'With man it is impossible; but with God all things are possible.' And the redeeming power of God is as available for a minority as for a majority: there is no restraint to the Lord to save by many or by few; and when working through a minority of people themselves redeemed and truly dedicated, it can work miracles. We see this happening again and again in Christian history; and it is because of our faith that it is so that we have courage to go on.

At the other end there is the power of man, the power of one man over another, or of men in society over other men in society, for his, for their, own selfish ends; and it is this which we are to redeem—to redeem *from*, to speak accurately, but we may also speak of redeeming *it*, the wrong use of power, may speak of the redemption of power. How to relate our Christian Pacifist convictions to the sphere of government, of the State, with its elements—all so antipathetic to our highest insights—of justice, compulsion and compromise, is a problem which we have hardly begun to touch. Any plea for a Tolstoyan anarchism is, I believe, a fruitless line; but I do not pretend to have any of the answers myself. I only wish to urge that here, where the greatest challenge lies to our effective thinking, we must still go out from the same centre. The State, government, power in the political and economic sense, must be brought within the compass of the redemption which is the deepest motive behind all our pacifism. Somehow we must learn to let the healing power of God work through us for the redemption of power as men, and as nations, know power. 'And Jesus called them to him and saith unto them: Ye know that they who are accounted to rule over the nations lord it over them, and their great ones tyrannize over them. But so shall it not be among you. But whosoever will be great among you shall wait upon you; and whosoever of you will be the first shall be everyone's slave. For even the Son of Man came not to be waited on but to do the waiting; and to give his life, to redeem many.' Somewhere *there* lies the redemption of power to which our pacifism must be dedicated if it is to be His: to be *Christ*ian Pacifism. I do not pretend to have the answers, or to offer applications and details; but the secret lies somewhere there.

NOTES

[1] I have tried to draw this out in my essay, 'The Church's Ministry of Suffering', in *Studies in Christian Social Commitment*, ed. J. Ferguson.

[2] p. 104; I have ventured to reverse the order of the phrases in the last two contrasting pairs.

[3] E. Grubb, *Thoughts on the Divine in Man*, pp. 12 f.

[4] p. 3.

[5] p. 11.

[6] *op. cit.*, p. 9.

[7] For a recent presentation of this, see the inaugural lecture by the present Spalding Professor of Eastern Religions at Oxford, R. C. Zaehner, *Foolishness to the Greeks*.

[8] *A. Neave Brayshaw*, ed. R. Davis and R. C. Wilson, p. 59.

[9] W. R. Maltby, *Christ and His Cross*, p. 66.

INDEX

BT 736.4 .N8 1971
Nuttall, Geoffrey F.
1911-2007.
Christian pacifism in

84

Sawtr

WORLD WITHOUT WAR COUNCIL OF THE UNITED STATES

The principle objectives of the Council are:

Establishing the goal of ending war as a guiding force in American life;

Clarifying realistic strategies and defining specific tasks essential to achieving that goal;

Engaging the leaders of private organizations and institutions in appropriate work through their own constituencies to translate these strategies into public policy;

Offering through national and regional intelligence and action centers the catalytic, training, publishing, programming and coordinating services needed;

Demonstrating models of continuing work in the climate-setting sectors of American life (e.g., mass media, education, labor, business, religion, scientific);

Providing a continuing overview of the American peace effort designed to counter the waste and futility of many past efforts by common attempts to develop standards for effective work.

Write for full information on current programs, publications and work opportunities.

World Without War Council Offices

National: Office of the President, 1730 Grove Street, Berkeley, California 94709
Office of the Chairman of the Board, 838 Fifth Avenue, New York, N. Y. 10003
Midwest: 7245 South Merrill, Chicago, Illinois 60649
Northwest: 1514 N. E. 45th Street, Seattle, Washington 98105
Eugene: 119 E. 10th Avenue, Eugene, Oregon 97401
Portland: 215 S. E. 9th Avenue, Portland, Oregon 97214
Pacific Central: 1730 Grove Street, Berkeley, California 94709